Top 25 locator map
(continues on inside
back cover)

◄

TwinPack
Crete

SUSIE BOULTON

Susie Boulton first got to know
Crete on a Greek island-
hopping holiday over 20
years ago. Since then she has
written travel features and
contributions to guide books
on the island. A graduate of
Cambridge University, where
she studied languages
and history of art, she is a
freelance travel writer and
author of guide books to
Venice, Lisbon, the Algarve,
Malta and other European
destinations.

If you have any comments
or suggestions for this guide
you can contact the editor at
Twinpacks@theAA.com

AA Publishing
Find out more about AA Publishing
and the wide range of travel publications
and services the AA provides by visiting
our website at www.theAA.com/travel

Contents

About this book

TwinPack Crete is divided into six sections to cover the six most important aspects of your visit to Crete. It includes:

- The author's view of the island and its people
- Suggested walks and excursions
- The Top 25 sights to visit
- The best of the rest – aspects of the island that make it special
- Detailed listings of restaurants, hotels, shops and nightlife
- Practical information

In addition, easy-to-read side panels provide fascinating extra facts and snippets, highlights of places to visit and invaluable practical advice.

CROSS-REFERENCES
To help you make the most of your visit, cross-references, indicated by ➤ show you where to find additional information about a place or subject.

MAPS
The fold-out map in the wallet at the back of the book is a large-scale island map of Crete.

The Top 25 locator maps found on the inside front and back covers of the book itself are for quick reference. They show the Top 25 sights, described on pages 24–48, which are clearly plotted by number (**1** – **25**, not page number) in alphabetical order.

PRICES
Where appropriate, an indication of the cost of an establishment is given by € signs: €€€ denotes higher prices, €€ denotes average prices, while € denotes lower prices.

CRETE
life

A Personal View

More than any other island in the Mediterranean, Crete has the power to arouse the imagination. Ancient ruins and the exquisite works of art they have revealed offer a tantalising glimpse of Europe's first great civilisation: the highly sophisticated Minoans who built the great palace of Knossós, alleged home of King Minos and the Minotaur. The ruins of a Dorian city-state, the mighty ramparts of Venetian fortresses, the soaring minarets of Ottoman mosques, all survive as eloquent evidence of later foreign powers, lured by the island's strategic maritime setting.

Steeped in myth, history and traditions, Crete is also an island of golden beaches and blue seas which has grown to cater for an annual invasion of 2 million visitors. The sands of the north are now skirted by high-rise development, yet in the south small, remote settlements are tucked between spectacular cliffs and the Libyan Sea, some only accessible by ferry or fishing boat. Untouched too is the spectacular mountainous interior of the island where locals go by donkey, Byzantine churches glow with frescoes and rustic villages are lost in time.

Fiercely proud, with a passion for freedom and independence, the islanders regard themselves

Cascades of flowers on terraced houses in the old town of Réthymno

first as Cretans, secondly as Greeks. Relaxed and friendly, they will readily offer the visitor a glass of *rakí*, a slice of raisin bread or a bunch of grapes. It is this warm hospitality, combined with ancient history, natural beauty and sparkling seas, that make the island, quite simply, unforgettable.

Top: *outside the barber's shop*

Bottom: *keeping guard in Haniá's market*

This proud and unyielding character has been moulded by many years of sieges, battles and famines; but the warmth and hospitality of the people are shaped, above all, by the Mediterranean climate. Long mornings are followed by a leisurely lunch and a siesta of two or three hours. Business resumes until about 8pm when it is time for the *vólta* or evening stroll. If there's one thing the locals love it's a fiesta, and they enthusiastically participate in saints' days and other religious festivals. Visitors to the island are more than welcome to join in.

Crete in Figures

GEOGRAPHY
- Crete is long and thin, extending 250km from east to west and varying from 12km to 60km from north to south.
- Crete has 1,046km of coastline.
- Apart from the tiny outpost of Gávdos, Crete is the most southerly of the Greek islands.
- Crete has about 300 days of sunshine a year.

POPULATION
- The population of Crete is 550,000.
- Roughly half the population live in the administrative district of Iráklio, a quarter in Haniá and an eighth in both Réthymno and Lassíthi.
- Most of the population live on the north coast.

GOVERNMENT
- Crete is an administrative district of Greece, and sends elected deputies to the Athens' parliament.
- The island is divided into four provinces: Haniá, Réthymno, Iráklio and Lassíthi.
- Each province has a governor, appointed by the Greek Government in Athens.

TOURISM
- Tourism is overtaking agriculture as the main source of income. Exports of fruit and vegetables are on the decline as more and more coastal villages turn to tourism.
- Of the 2 million plus tourists that visit Crete annually, the majority are German, followed by Scandinavians and British.
- Crete's tourist season currently lasts only seven months. Crete is keen to benefit from a longer season by embarking on a winter pilot programme with emphasis on sports, health benefits, cultural and ecological pursuits.

Walking off the ferry from Agía Rouméli

People of Crete

El Greco

Doménico Theotokópoulos (*c*1541–1614), more familiarly known as El Greco, was born in Crete in about *c*1541. As a young artist he went to Venice and studied under Titian, then moved to Rome where he came under the influence of Michelangelo, Raphael and the Mannerists of central Italy. From 1577 El Greco lived in Spain, working mainly in Toledo. He is best known for his passionate and often disturbing Mannerist paintings. See also Fódele ➤ 58.

Detail from a statue of Níkos Kazantzákis, Crete's most celebrated writer

Níkos Kazantzákis

The writer and poet Níkos Kazantzákis (1883–1957) was born in Iráklio but spent most of his life abroad. Regarded as the leading Greek writer of his time, he produced novels, travel journals, poetry and philosophical essays, as well as translating western classics into modern Greek. His best known novels, both set in Crete, are *Zorba the Greek*, which became a famous film, and *Freedom or Death*. In 1957 he narrowly missed being awarded the Nobel Prize for Literature. He died in Germany a few months later and is buried on the old town walls of Iráklio. See also Myrtía ➤ 60.

Sir Arthur Evans

The British archaeologist Sir Arthur Evans (1851–1941) came to Crete in 1894, intrigued by the discovery on the island of ancient coins and stone seals with pictographics. With an inherited fortune he bought the site of Knossós (➤ 38) and in 1900 began his excavations. Major discoveries were immediately made, causing a sensation throughout Europe. Evans devoted the rest of his life to Knossós, publishing his research in the six-volume work, *The Palace of Minos*. His reconstructions of the palace have incited much controversy, but his work has greatly advanced the study of European prehistory. Evans bequest of the site to the British School of Archaeology in Athens and their gift of it to Greece secured for the Greeks a fundamental part of their history that subsequently proved to be one of the most visited and remunerative sites in the world.

ZEUS
Mythical Zeus, King of the Greek Gods, is Crete's ancient hero. Born in the Díkti Cave (➤ 50), he led a revolt against the Titans, dethroned his father Kronos (King of the Titans), and divided the world. His brothers Hades and Poseidon were given the underworld and the seas respectively, while Zeus kept the heavens, becoming the God of the Universe.

A Chronology

6000BC	Arrival of Crete's first inhabitants, probably from Asia Minor or the Levant. The main settlement of these neolithic people is Knossós.
3000BC *Start of the Bronze Age*	Beginnings of the great Minoan civilisation, known as the Pre-Palatial period. Ceramics, tools, weapons and jewellery produced by craftsmen.
2200BC	Start of Middle Minoan or Proto-Palatial period. First appearance of pictographic script.
2000–1800BC	Construction of the first palaces at Knossós, Phaestós, Mália and Zákros.
1700BC	A natural catastrophe destroys the first palaces of the Minoan civilisation, but new ones are built on their foundations, marking the Neo-Palatial period.
c1450BC	Palaces and towns destroyed by an unknown disaster. Knossós partially destroyed, but reoccupied. Mycenaeans invade Crete.
1370BC	Final destruction of Knossós, probably by Mycenaeans.
1100BC *Start of the Iron Age*	Dorian invasions. End of Bronze Age and start of urban civilisations.
Late 4th century BC to 1st century AD	Hellenistic period (323BC) and Classical Age (500BC) – Cretan cities vie with each other.
67BC	Romans complete conquest of Crete; Górtys becomes the new capital.
AD47	St Paul driven ashore during his journey to Rome; Crete is soon converted to Christianity.
330	Division of the Roman Empire; Crete passes to the Eastern Empire under Byzantium.
824	The Saracen Arabs take Crete.
961	The Byzantine Empire reconquers Crete.
1204	Crete passes to Venice after the Venetian conquest of Constantinople during the Fourth Crusade.

1210	Venetians make Candia (now Iráklio) their Cretan capital.
1645	The Ottomans attack Crete, capturing Haniá and Réthymno.
1669	Candia surrenders after a seige lasting 22 years and two months. Venetians evacuate the island.
1821	Cretan uprising against the Ottomans during the Greek War of Independence (1821–30).
1866	Several hundred Cretans, under siege by Turkish troops, die heroically – along with many of their aggressors – in the explosion at Moní Arkadíou.
1878	First excavations at the Palace of Knossós by Mínos Kalokairinós, a Cretan businessman.
1897–98	Crete and Greece unite against the Ottoman (Turkish) military who are ejected from the island. Crete becomes autonomous.
1900	Sir Arthur Evans begins excavations at Knossós. Work also begins at the Phaestós site.
1913	Crete is annexed to mainland Greece as part of the terms of the Treaty of London.
1941	Battle of Crete. German airborne invasion of the island. Heavy losses on both sides.
1945	Germans withdraw from the island followed by the Liberation of Crete.
1960s	Tourist boom begins. Hotels are constructed on the north coast. From 1967–74 Greece is under a military dictatorship.
1986	Greece becomes a full member of the EC, and funds are used for improving the infrastructure, such as. roads, hospitals and the the restoration of Cretan churches, monasteries and monuments.
2004	The Olympic Games is hosted by Greece for the first time since 1896. Some events are staged in Iráklio.

Best of Crete

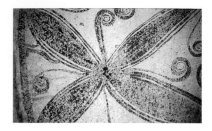

Intricate Minoan decoration

ESSENTIAL INFORMATION TO GET THE BEST FROM YOUR VISIT

Opening times for museums, archaeological sites and, to a lesser extent monasteries, are impossible to predict. They vary from season to season; closing earlier in the winter or not opening at all. Frequent strikes and regular personnel shortages can lead to shorter opening hours and a change of central government can also have an effect.

Generally it is advisable to visit in the mornings, but most sites are closed on Monday mornings; if not all day. Many sites are open to about 3pm in the summer (1pm, if they are open in the winter), but monasteries could close earlier for a siesta. Major sites, such as Knossós and Phaestós are generally open every day from 8.30am to 7pm (except in the winter).

If you wish to visit a particular site it is best to telephone in advance or get up-to-date information from your hotel reception, travel representative or local tourist office.

If you only have a short time to visit Crete, or would like to get a complete picture of the island, here are the essentials:

• Learn about Minoan civilisation on Crete by soaking up the atmosphere of the palace of Knossós (➤ 38) then viewing the wonderful displays in Iráklio's Archaeological Museum (➤ 28).

• Wander around Haniá (➤ 35), one of Crete's most attractive towns, then take some time to relax in a café or taverna looking out over the picturesque harbour.

• Join in the dancing at a typical Cretan evening in a country taverna – an impromptu event with the locals is best, but even those that have been staged for tourists offer an infectious brand of Cretan fun.

• Hike down the spectacular Samariá Gorge – a demanding, but almost compulsory day out (➤ 33).

• Conjure up images of marauding pirates at the Venetian fortress in Réthymno (➤ 46), then explore the ancient streets.

• Head for the hills, and discover absolute seclusion amid magnificent scenery in one of the rugged mountain ranges – the Lefká Óri (White Mountains), the Ída Mountains or the Díkti massif.

• Take a boat trip around the coast to see otherwise inaccessible beaches and coves, or take a ferry or caïque to an offshore island.

• Savour a simple meal of freshly caught fish and a glass or two of Cretan wine, while gazing out over the sea from a taverna with a view.

• Go to market (➤ 76) in Iráklio or Haniá and be tempted by the enormous range of herbs, spices, *rakí* and honey – the perfect place to make up a picnic.

• Take to the streets at festival time (➤ 22) – there are plenty of opportunities throughout the year to see colourful processions, fireworks and Cretans having a good time.

Crete
how to organise your time

13

A Walk in Ágios Nikólaos

This walk begins at the harbour in the centre of the resort (► 26).

From the harbour walk up the tamarisk-lined Odós Roussou Koundoúrou, one of the two main shopping streets. Take the first street to the left, Odós Sfakianáki.

INFORMATION

Distance 1.8km
Time 2 hours
Start point Harbour
End point Lake Voulisméni
Lunch Café du Lac (€€)
  ✉ By the lake
  ☎ 28410 22414

Towards the far end of Odós Sfakianáki there are splendid views of the Gulf of Merabéllo. The marina below was constructed in 1994.

At the end of the street, turn left to climb some steps, then make your way down to the water-front. Here, turn left, passing Kitroplatía Beach, and continue along the water-front until you come to the harbour.

Soak up the atmosphere of the harbour with a drink in one of the waterside cafés. The boats and cruisers moored here offer fishing, swimming and glass-bottom boat trips, excursions to Spinalónga Island, (► 30) and evening tours of the bay.

Make for the bridge on the west corner of the harbour and the small Folk Museum. Walk up the steep Odós Palaiológou for a visit to the Archaeological Museum, then retrace your steps down to the lake on your right.

Scenic view from between the buildings in Ágios Nikólaos

The 64m-deep Lake Voulisméni, encircled by fishing boats and flanked by cliffs on its western side, was origi-nally believed to be bottomless. In 1867 it was linked to the harbour by a channel and cleared of its stagnant waters. Today it is a tourist magnet, the lakeview cafés luring customers with their tempting range of exotic ices and cocktails. For the best views take the steps up at the far side, beyond the Café du Lac.

A Walk around Haniá

Start at the Naval Museum (► 53), which is situated on the west side of the Old Harbour.

With the water on your right, walk along the exterior of the fortifications and cut inland along Odós Theotokopoúlou, a picturesque street with old Venetian houses and craft shops. At the end, turn left down Odós Zambelíou and at the main square turn right.

Hálidon, a street lined with shops, is the tourist hub of Haniá. On the right is the Archaeological Museum (► 52) and just beyond it, in the courtyard of the Catholic church, the small Folk Museum. On the other side of the road are the poorly restored Turkish baths (new tourist shops!) and a large square overlooked by Haniá's cathedral.

INFORMATION

Distance 2.5km
Time 2–3 hours including sightseeing
Start end/point Venetian harbour
Lunch Michális Tavérna (€€–€€€) ✉ Aktí Tobázi 54–56, Old Harbour
☎ 28210 58330

Take the second left for Odós Skrídlof, a narrow alley packed with leather stalls, and go straight on for the covered market. Continuing along the same road, take the second street on the left for the delightful 16th-century Ágii Anágyri, housing ancient icons.

At end of the street the tree-lined Plateía 1821 is overlooked by Ágios Nikólaos, a former monastery church that was later coverted into a mosque and retaining its soaring minaret.

At the opposite side of the square turn right for the Inner Harbour. Divert left along Odós Kaneváro to see the Greek/Swedish excavations that have revealed Minoan remains.

Flower garden outside Haniá's covered market

At the waterfront, on the right, are the vaults of the 16th century Venetian arsenals. Fish tavernas overlook the colourful Inner Harbour. From here you can walk along the jetty to the lighthouse, or turn left to return to the Old Harbour, passing the Mosque of the Janissaries.

A Walk around Iráklio

INFORMATION

Distance 3km
Time 2–5 hours depending on visits
Start point Plateía Eleftherías
End point Harbour
Lunch Ippókampos (€)
    ☒ Odós Sófokli Venizélou
    ☎ 2810 280240

Start at Plateía Eleftherías (Freedom Square), a traffic-encircled hub of the city with gardens and cafés. North of the square visit Iráklio's famous Archaeological Museum (► 28).

West of Plateía Eleftherías take Odós Daidálos, a pedestrian shopping thoroughfare leading to Plateía Venizélos, the heart of the city.
Try *bougátsa*, a pastry speciality, in one of the cafés overlooking the Morozíni Fountain.

Facing Odós Daidálos, turn right and make for the market (► 76) in Odós 1866 on the far side of the crossroads. In the square at the end of the street a café occupies a hexagonal building which was formerly a Turkish fountain; the nearby Venetian Bembo fountain (1588) was assembled with a headless Roman statue and other antiquities.

The remains of the Venetian Arsenali in Iráklio make a shady retreat

Returning along Odós 1866, take the second street on your left, and at the end turn right and then left over Odós 1821 to bring you into Plateía Aikaterínis. The square is dominated by the huge neo-Byzantine Cathedral of Ágios Minás (1895). In its shadow lies the original, more charming Ágios Minás, with a splen-did iconostatis. On the near side, Agía Ekateríni houses a fine collection of icons (► 24).

Turn right off the square for the busy Odós Kalokairinoú and right again. A left turn at the crossroads will bring you back to the Morozíni Fountain. Cross the square for Odós 25 Avgoústou. On the right is Ágios Márkos (St Mark's church) and further on the reconstructed arcaded Loggia (today the Town Hall) was the meeting-place for Venetian nobil-ity. Just beyond lies Ágios Títos on its own square.

Continue down the street for the harbour and Venetian fortress (► 36).

A Walk through the Samariá Gorge

Start at the tourist pavilion at the head of the gorge. Hikers should come equipped with sturdy footwear, sunhat, sunscreen and refreshments (there are drinking points and streams along the gorge but no food).

Take the stairway known as the *xilóskala* (wooden stairs) which drops steeply, descending 1,000m in the first 2km.

The first landmark is the tiny Church of Ágios Nikólaos, shaded by pines and cypresses.

The path narrows as you reach the bottom of the gorge (4km from the start). In summer the river is reduced to a mere trickle.

The half-way point, and a good spot for a picnic, is the abandoned village of Samariá. The inhabitants were rehoused in the early 1960s when the area became a national park. To the east of the gorge lies the small 14th-century Church of Óssia María, containing original frescoes. The church gave its name to the village and gorge.

Follow the narrowing trail between towering cliffs, crossing the river at various points. Continue walking until you see a small church on the left.

Beyond the sanctuary built by the Sfakiots, you can see ahead the famous *sideróportes* or Iron Gates, the narrowest point of the walk. The corridor narrows to a mere 3m, the towering walls either side rising to 300m.

Beyond the gates, the path opens out and you walk down the valley to the coast.

At the old abandoned village of Agía Rouméli, a drinks kiosk is a welcome sight.

Continue to the modern coastal village of Agía Rouméli where tavernas, the cool sea water and the ferry back to civilisation await.

INFORMATION

Distance 16km
Time 5–7 hours
🕐 May to mid-Oct
   (mid-Apr to Oct weather
   permitting)
Start point Omalós Plain,
   43km south of Haniá
End point Agía Rouméli
⛴ Ferries to Hóra Sfakíon,
   where there are buses
   back to Haniá. Also ferries
   to Soúgia and Palaeóchora.
   Check times of the last
   boats and buses. Guided
   tours available through
   any travel agent.
Lunch Tavernas at the top of
   the gorge and in Agía
   Rouméli (€–€€);
   a picnic is recommended
   for the gorge

Welcoming water stop down the Samariá Gorge

A Drive Around Akrotíri Peninsula

From Haniá take the airport road, turning left at the top of the hill for the Venizélos Graves. Stone slabs mark the graves of Elefthérios Venizélos (1864–1936), Crete's famous statesman and his son, Sophoklís. The site has a magnificent view of Haniá, mountains and coast.

INFORMATION

Distance 45km
Time Half a day, including sightseeing
Start end/point Haniá
Lunch Kalathás (€–€€)
✉ Kalathás beach, Kalathás
☎ 28210 64729

Continue on the airport road, then follow signs for Agía Triáda. The Venetian-influenced 17th-century monastery has a church with a fine Renaissance façade, and a peaceful courtyard with fruit trees. A small shop sells olive oil and wine made by the monks and a museum houses a collection of icons, reliquaries and vestments.

From Agía Triáda, walk or drive along the asphalt road through rocky, barren hills to the Gouvernétou Monastery (4.5km). This isolated monastery, founded in 1548, also shows a strong

Venetian influence. From the monastery a path (about 30 minutes' walk) leads down to a beautiful gorge with the ruins of the Katholikó Monastery and Cave of St John the Hermit (torch needed). Pilgrims come here on 7 October each year to celebrate the Saint's Day.

Retrace the route to Agía Triáda, and, at the end of the tree-lined avenue, turn right onto the road for Horafákia (3km). Then drive straight through the village of Stavrós. The beautiful circular bay of pale sands and calm, aquamarine waters provided the setting for the final scenes in the film *Zorba the Greek*.

Tribute at the grave of Elefthérios Venizélos

Return to Horafákia and in the village turn right for Haniá. Reaching the coast, stop at Kalathás Beach. One of the prettiest beaches on the peninsula, this is a good spot for a swim and a meal before the return journey to Haniá.

A Drive Around the Lassíthi Plateau

The tour starts from Neápoli (➤ 60) but can also be approached from Ágios Nikólaos or the north coast. It is important to take non-slip shoes and a torch for the caves.

Follow the sign for Lassíthi from the main square in Neápoli. The road twists its way scenically up through the mountains.
Stop at the café at Zénia for a break from the bends and a breathtaking view of the Díkti peaks.

Continue up through villages where locals sell wine, *rakí* and honey by the roadside.
After about 27km, the plateau comes suddenly and spectacularly into view. Stop by the roadside to look down on to the flat plain, encircled by soaring mountains. Look up towards the mountains for a possibly sighting of a bird of prey.

After the village of Mesa Lassíthi, turn right at the road junction for Tzermiádo (signposted to Dzermido).

Signed from the main road, the Krónio Cave (also known as the Cave of Trápeza) was used as a burial site from prehistoric times. Around 1km from the parking area, there are (optional) guides to show you the way.

Continue along the road encircling the plateau. At the junction at Pinakianó go straight on, following signs for Psychró. Beyond the village of Pláti, follow signs for the Díkti Cave.
This is Crete's most famous cave (➤ 50), the so-called birthplace of Zeus.

Continue around the plateau until you reach the village of Ágios Geórgios which has a folk museum, well signed from the centre.

At Ágios Konstantínos the full circle of the plateau has been completed. Turn right to return to Neápoli. This is a pleasant, non-touristy, town to have a drink or a meal – try Yéfseis Restaurant in the main square.

INFORMATION

Distance 83km
Time 6–7 hours, including stops and lunch
Start/end point Neápoli
Lunch Krónio (€)
    ✉ Tzermiádo
    ☎ 28440 22375

Walking up the stony path towards the entrance to the Díkti Cave

19

Finding Peace & Quiet

PEACE AND QUIET

VULTURE SPOTTING

Birdwatchers should look out for the rare lammergeirer, an eagle-like vulture that inhabits mountainous regions. It is not hard to recognise, with a wing span of nearly 3m and a wedge-shaped tail.

Crete's varied landscape, from coastal plains to mountain plateaux and peaks, provides endless prospects for nature-lovers and walkers. Botanists flock to the island in March and April, when the slopes and coastal strips are covered with wild flowers; birdwatchers come to see migratory species in spring and rare birds of prey throughout the year. Walkers have a choice of ancient rural footpaths, spectacular gorge walks and serious hikes in the mountains. Those in search of peace and quiet should avoid the summer months, when tourism is at its height. This is also the time when the landscape is parched by the intense heat of the sun.

FLORA

Thanks to its southern Mediterranean climate and variety of habitat, Crete has an extraordinary diversity of plant life. There are over 1,500 species, a significant number of which are indigenous to the island. In spring, hills and mountain slopes are a carpet of wild flowers: yellow anenomes, pink and white cistus, blue campanulas, wild irises, orchids and clematis; on the coast there are poppies, stocks and small campions; in the fields flax, poppies, asphodels and wild tulips. In summer the land is hot and lifeless, but autumn brings flowering cyclamen, autumn crocus and sea squill. The Samariá Gorge (➤ 33) is particularly rich in plant life, including the Cretan cyclamen, the clusius peony and the Cretan ebony, a shrub unique to Crete with beautiful pinkish-purple flowers. Much of the landscape consists of *phrígana*, the equivalent of the French *garigue* – a stony, open habitat of scrub and shrub, rich in wild flowers including the beautiful bee orchid and herbs such as oregano, marjoram, rosemary, sage and thyme.

Walk on the wild side at Préveli beach

The yellow horned poppy

BIRDS

Crete is a key stopping-off point for migrant species making their way from North Africa to their breeding grounds in northern Europe. The best months to see them are March, April and May. Where there are wetlands you may see migratory waders such as avocets, sandpipers and ringed plovers, as well as year-round resident species such as marsh harriers, herons, little egrets and oystercatchers. In the mountains eagles and vultures soar above valleys, gorges and plateaux.

High up on the island of Spinalónga

WALKING

Walking is one of the best ways of seeing the island. Easily the most popular walk is the Samariá Gorge (➤ 17), open from May to October, but it is not for those who are seeking solitude. The Lefká Óri (White Mountains) in the west of the island and the Psiloreítis range, southwest of Iráklio, offer the best mountain walks. Specialist companies offer organised half-day or day-long walks with an experienced guide (➤ 83), and serious climbers can contact the mountaineering clubs (➤ 83). If you're planning your own walk in the mountains you'll need suitable footwear, a hat, sunscreen, a whistle and extra water. You should also take a map and compass and know how to use them. The best time for walking is April and May when the weather is warm, but not too hot, and wild flowers adorn the wayside. Autumn is good too, though the countryside is less rewarding.

21

What's On

JANUARY *New Year's Day* (1 Jan): processions, traditional seasonal songs and cutting of the New Year's Cake. *Epiphany* (6 Jan): blessings of the water; crosses thrown into the sea.

MARCH *Kathará Deftéra* 'Clean Monday' (last Monday before Lent): celebrations marking the end of Carnival and beginning of Lent. *Independence Day* (25 Mar): military parades. *Holy Week:* Greek Orthodox Easter falls up to four weeks either side of the Western festival. This is the most important religious festival in Greece.

MAY *Labour Day* (1 May): parades and flower festivals. Commemorations of the Battle of Crete (20–27 May), celebrated in Haniá.

JULY Festivals and folk performances all over Crete; local tourist offices have information. *Cretan Wine Festival* (mid-Jul): a week of wine tasting and dancing in Réthymno.

AUGUST Fair in Anógia (6 Aug). *Sultana Festival* (mid-Aug), in Sitía. *Feast of the Assumption* (15 Aug). Pilgrimage for those named Ioánnis (John) to the Church of Ágios Ioánnis on the Rodopoú peninsula, Haniá (29 Aug). *Summer in Haniá*: music, dance, shows. *Renaissance Festival:* music, drama and films at the Venetian fortress in Réthymno.

OCTOBER *Chestnut Festival* (mid-Oct), in Élos and other villages of southwest Crete. *Óchi Day* ('No' Day, 28 Oct): commemorating the day the Greeks turned down Mussolini's ultimatum in World War II.

NOVEMBER Commemoration in Réthymno and Arkádi of the destruction of the Arkádi monastery in 1866 by the Turks (7–9 Nov). *Feast of the Presentation of the Virgin in the Temple* (21 Nov), in Réthymno.

DECEMBER *Christmas Day* (25 Dec): feast day, but less significant to the Cretans than Easter.

CRETE's
top 25 sights

The sights are shown on the maps on the inside front cover and inside back cover, numbered **1**–**25** alphabetically

Agía Ekateríni, Iráklio

INFORMATION

✚ D2
✉ Plateía Ekaterínis
☎ 2810 288825
🕐 Check for times
🍴 Cafés (€) in Plateía Ekaterínis
♿ 2 shallow steps, otherwise no problem
💶 Moderate

If you are interested in icons, then you should visit this 16th-century church located in the same square as Iráklio's cathedral.

Within the Church of Agía Ekateriní (St Catherine), the Museum of Religious Art houses the most important collection of icons in Crete. During the 16th and 17th centuries the church was part of the Mount Sinai Monastery School, which became one of the centres of the 'Cretan Renaissance'. The style of painting was characterised by the intermingling of Byzantine iconography with elements inspired by the Western Renaissance.

One of the pupils here was Mikhaíl Damaskinós, and the six icons by him produced for the Vrondísi Monastery near Zarós, that are central to the collection and on the right as you go in, are the finest works of art in the museum. They have been located in the church since the early 19th century; a wise move as the Turks destroyed just about everything of artistic importance in the monastery in the 1860s. Doménico Theotokópoulos, more commonly known as El Greco (➤ 9), may have been one of his contemporaries here.

Bust of the celebrated painter El Greco

Among other students were the writers Vitzéntzos Kornários and Yeórghios Hortátzis, who also contributed to the 'Cretan Renaissance'. The building was used as a mosque during Turkish rule.

Agía Triáda (Minoan Summer Palace)

Linked to Phaestós by paved road, the dramatically sited Agía Triáda is believed to have been the summer palace of Minoan royalty.

Close to the more famous Minoan palace of Phaestós (➤ 45), Agía Triáda enjoys an equally if not more spectacular setting, on a slope overlooking the Bay of Mesarás. Far fewer tourists come here, and it is a delightful spot to explore. There is no record of the Minoan name ('Agía Triáda' is the name of a nearby Byzantine chapel) and the purpose of another palace so close to Phaestós remains a mystery. The setting, which in Minoan times would have been far closer to the sea, and the elaborate decoration of the apartments, suggest this was a luxurious summer villa, possibly for use by the royalty of Phaestós. The original 'palace' was razed to the ground in the disaster of 1450BC (➤ 10) and was not rebuilt until some 200 years later.

The best starting point is the Byzantine chapel. From here you can look down on the complex: to the left the grandest, sea-view apartments, which had flagstoned floors, gypsum and alabaster-faced walls, and in the corner room, fine frescoes. To the right is a group of storerooms with *pithoi* (large storage jars) and further to the right the main reception rooms. On the far side of the palace lie the ruins of a town with a porticoed row of shops.

Some of the most exquisite Minoan works of art in Iráklio's Archaeological Museum (➤ 28) were found here. These include three carved black stone vases (the Harvester Vase, Boxer Vase and the Chieftain Cup) and a painted sarcophagus depicting a burial procession.

INFORMATION

✚ C2
✉ 3km west of Phaestós
☎ 28920 91360
🕐 Check for times
🍴 Café (€) at Phaestós
🚌 Buses only as far as Phaestós (3km)
♿ None (many steps, not suitable)
💶 Moderate
↔ Phaestós (➤ 45), Museum of Cretan Ethnology at Vóri (➤ 47)

Church ruins at Agía Triáda

Ágios Nikólaos

From a peaceful little harbour town, Ágios Nikólaos has grown into one of the most popular and lively resorts on Crete.

In the Hellenistic era this was the port for Lató, whose archaeological remains can be seen in the hills to the west (► 54). The town fell into decline under the Romans but was later developed by the Venetians, who built a fort dominating the Gulf of Merabéllo (Beautiful View). In 1303 this was damaged by an earthquake, then later razed to the ground by the Turks. In 1870 Sfakiots from western Crete settled at the port, naming it after the Byzantine church of Ágios Nikólaos to the north. The town today may not boast the architectural features and historic background of Crete's other regional capitals; nonetheless it is a picturesque resort with a lively atmosphere that appeals to all ages. There is nothing particularly Cretan about it, and the chief attraction is, and always has been, the setting on a hilly promontory overlooking the deep blue Gulf of Merabéllo.

In the centre of the resort, tavernas and cafés cluster around the busy fishing harbour and the deep-water Lake Voulisméni, which is linked to the harbour by a short canal. By day the main activity is strolling around the quaysides, browsing in the shops and taking leisurely lunches. Evening life centres on bars with music, cafés with cocktails and half a dozen discos. Luxury hotels provide pristine beaches, but public bathing areas leave much to be desired but you can walk or take a bus to the sandy beach of Almirós, 2km to the south.

The picturesque harbour at Ágios Nikólaos

Áptera

The location of Áptera is one of the most impressive in Crete and excavations now reveal the most important post-Minoan site in western Crete.

Áptera contains Dorian, Classical and Hellenistic Greek and Roman remains together with a Venetian monastic settlement and a Turkish fort – a full cross section of Cretan history. The new excavations at the west gate have uncovered some extremely interesting tomb structures and the recently exposed pillared peristyle hall to a luxurious Graeco-Roman villa that collapsed in an earthquake is virtually complete. The imposing Roman cisterns are some of the most outstanding examples of Roman engineering anywhere in Europe. This powerful walled city controlled the entrance to Soúda bay and was inhabited from around 1000BC. It was destroyed by an earthquake in AD700 and was sacked by the Saracen Arabs in AD824.

Áptera means 'wingless one' and is said to have taken its name from a musical contest between the Muses and the Sirens. The Sirens were so dejected at being defeated that they plucked off their wings and jumped into the sea; hence the islands in the bay below. Sadly Áptera was plundered like most archaeological sites on Crete and in the mid-19th century a large proportion of the stone was used in the building of the Turkish fort and the Itzedin fortress at Kalámi. Many of the fine statues were broken up and put into lime kilns and the museum of Istanbul contains a host of the discoveries from Áptera including gilt statues of Roman emperors. However today the Archaeological Museum of Haniá (▶ 52) boasts a fine display of artefacts from this incredibly important site.

INFORMATION

➕ B1
✉ Close to Megála Horáfia, 12km east of Haniá.
☎ No phone
🕐 Check with tourist information in Haniá (▶ 35)
🚌 No bus service
♿ None
💷 Free

The Turkish fortress above the ancient site of Áptera

Archaiologikó Mouseío, Iráklio

INFORMATION

- D2
- Plateía Elefthérias (entrance on Odós Xanthoudídou), Iráklio
- 2810 224630
- Check for times
- Cafeteria (€) beside the museum
- Bus stop by the museum
- Opposite the museum
- Ground floor only
- Expensive; free on Sun in winter
- A visit to Knossós (➤ 38) before or after a tour of the museum (ideally both) will give a more complete picture of the Minoan civilisation

The bull's head rhyton in Iráklio's museum

Iráklio's Archaeological Museum contains the world's richest collection of Minoan art, providing a vivid insight into the life of a highly cultured society.

The museum has a wonderful collection of archaeological finds that span ten centuries, from early Neolithic to Roman times; but the main emphasis is on the Minoan era, with treasures from Knossós, Phaestós and other ancient palaces of Crete. The dreary 1960's museum building hardly does justice to this remarkable collection, and the sparse labelling and information makes the purchase of a guide book essential. However, the wealth of exhibits warrants more than one visit, perhaps concentrating on the ground floor galleries in the morning and the upstairs Hall of Frescoes later in the day.

The range of exhibits is enormous, from votive figurines, seal stones, cult vessels and gold jewellery to spearheads and sarcophagi. Among the individual highlights are the Phaestós Disc in Room III in a single case, the tiny faience figures of the bare-breasted Snake Goddesses (Case 50), the bull's head *rhyton* (Case 51) and the tiny ivory acrobat in mid-air (Case 56), all in Room IV; and the three carved *rhytons* from Agía Triáda in Room VII: the Chieftain Cup, the Harvester vase and the Boxer vase.

At first floor level is the Hall of Frescoes, which many regard as being the greatest form of Minoan artistic achievement. Most of this collection comes from the Palace of Knossós and although they have been heavily restored these frescoes go to the heart of Minoan life. Dating from 1600–1400BC the frescoes are depictions of man in harmony with nature, of ceremonies and worship and scenes of daily life.

Elafonísi

Despite its increasing popularity and crowds in high season, the beach at Elafonísi and the National Park adjacent to it, are well worth a visit.

The semi-tropical beach of Elafonísi is one of the finest in the whole of Crete, with its pink-tinged sands and vivid turquoise waters. The beach is remotely located in the southwest of the island and visitors who wish to reach it by car face a long drive and many hairpin bends.

However, it is no longer the undiscovered and idyllic haven it used to be – there are now several restaurants, two small hotels, rooms to rent and, in high season, tourist boats and buses crammed full with eager daytrippers. A more peaceful alternative to the main beach is the tiny island of Elafonísi, just offshore, which is reached by wading knee-deep through the turquoise waters. Here there is another idyllic beach, where the waters are clear, shallow and ideal for children.

INFORMATION

- 🔲 A2
- ✉ 6km south of Chrysoskalítissa
- 🍴 Several cafés and tavernas (€–€€)
- 🚌 Once a day from Haniá
- ⛴ Ferries from Palaeóchora
- ♿ None
- ↔ Moní Chrysoskalítissa (➤ 51)

Looking towards the clear water at Elafonísi Beach

Eloúnda & Spinalónga

A stunning setting and several luxury hotels makes Eloúnda one of Crete's most desirable resorts. The island of Spinalónga is an eerie contrast.

Eloúnda lies north of Ágios Nikólaos, reached by a road that snakes its way above the Gulf of Merabéllo, then drops scenically down to the centre of the resort. Life here focuses on the cafés and tavernas around the boat-filled harbour, and the long sandy beach stretching beyond.

Coming into the resort from Ágios Nikólaos, a sharp right turning off the main road leads to a causeway linking Eloúnda to the Spinalónga peninsula. From here you can see the submerged remains of Venetian salt pans and the sunken remnants of the Graeco-Roman city state of Oloús. The remains are barely visible but the peninsula is a pleasant place to stroll, with coastal paths and birdlife. A path beside the Canal Bar (just across the bridge) leads to a Byzantine mosaic, which is all that remains of an early Christian basilica.

Eloúnda's luxury accommodation, including Crete's finest hotel (Eloúnda Beach ➤ 73) is situated away from the centre, off the road going south to Ágios Nikólaos. In peaceful surroundings, the hotels have their own private beaches and take full advantage of the glorious views over the gulf.

The island of Spinalónga, reached by caïque, lies off shore and is dominated by its Venetian fortress, built in 1579 to protect the port of Eloúnda. A resistance movement operated here and it was not until 1715, 46 years after the Turkish conquest of the rest of Crete, that the fort finally surrendered. In 1903 the island was turned into a leper colony, where conditions were cruel and prison-like. In 1957 the colony was closed and today the island is uninhabited and the fortress and town are in ruins.

Falássarna

Winding down the hillside to the west coast, Falássarna's magnificent sweeping beach comes into view, stretching round to Cape Koutrí in the north.

In addition to the beautiful crescent of pale sands, laped by azure waters, Falássarna is also the site of an ancient city, the remains of which can be seen 2km north of the beach. (Follow the track for 1.5km beyond the last building.) Among the scattered remnants of the Hellenistic city-state are a 'throne' carved out of the rock, tombs, quarries, towers, water cisterns and the ruins of houses and storerooms. The remains centre around the harbour basin, its location some 100m inland showing clear evidence of the gradual shifting of the island. The English sea captain, T. A. B. Spratt was the first person to recognise that the pre-historic wave notch around the cliffs on the west coast were the result of this action. In the distant past Crete's west coast was uplifted by 6–9m, while parts of eastern Crete were submerged, including the sunken city of Oloús (► 30). Excavations of the ancient city are still in the early stages, and only a small portion of the harbour has been unearthed.

More remains lie at the top of Cape Koutrí, site of the acropolis. Close by, the less appealing – but economically necessary – plastic greenhouses produce off-season vegetables for export to mainland Greece.

INFORMATION

🖫 A1
✉ 8km northwest of Plátanos
🍴 Two tavernas above the beach (€–€€)
🚌 2 per day from Haniá
♿ None

Fine view above Falássarna

9

Farángi Ímbrou (Ímbros Gorge)

INFORMATION

➕ B2
✉ 54km southeast of Haniá
☉ May–Oct, depending on weather, 7am–sunset
🍴 Cafés in Ímbros (€)
🚌 Service from Haniá and Hóra Sfakión
♿ Not suitable
💷 Moderate
↔ Frangokástello (➤ 54), Loutró (➤ 59)
❓ Sturdy footwear and drinks recommended

Among the rocks in Ímbros Gorge

If you don't want to undertake the longer and more popular Samariá Gorge, this striking gorge, makes an excellent alternative.

North of Hóra Sfakión, the Ímbros Gorge is a small-scale version of the famous Samariá Gorge (➤ 33). Equally spectacular, with similar scenery, it is far more peaceful than Samariá. The gorge is about 8km long, and the walk takes from 2 to 3 hours, either uphill from the coast east of Hóra Sfakión, or downhill from Ímbros village at the beginning of the gorge. At the end you either have to walk to Hóra Sfakión, catch a bus or wait for a taxi in Komitádes. The walk can only be made between May and October since winter torrents render the gorge impassable.

This ancient route through the gorge still contains some excellent examples of the original cobbled donkey trail (*kalderími*). In May 1941 this gorge provided the sole escape route for the retreating allied army when some 12,000 weary survivors of the German invasion on the north coast withdrew to the south coast and the Libyan sea to await embarkation from Hóra Sfakión. During the nights of 28–31 May the Royal Navy managed to evacuate some three quarters of them; leaving the remainder to be taken prisoner and forced to march all the way back to the north coast again.

Farángi Samariás (Samariá Gorge)

Towering peaks, plunging depths and springs of clear water – a dramatic setting for a walk through one of Europe's longest and deepest canyons.

In high season up to 2,000 tourists a day walk the 16km gorge, making it the second most popular Cretan experience after Knossós. The flood of walkers, mostly on guided tours, kills any real sense of adventure but the stunning mountain scenery is well worth the effort of the 5–7 hour hike. The gorge was designated a National Park in 1962 in an attempt to preserve its wealth of flora and fauna. Most importantly the park was created to protect the famous Cretan wild goats (*agrimi*, also known as *kri kri*), shy, nimble-footed animals that are occasionally glimpsed in the gorge.

The starting point at the head of the gorge is on the mountain-ringed Omalós plain, and by far the best plan is to arrive by public transport, hike through the gorge to Agía Rouméli and take a ferry from here to Hóra Sfakión, then a bus back to Haniá, the nearest main resort. The walk can be quite demanding and there are mules, especially in the midday sun, and a helicopter on hand to help those in trouble. Sturdy shoes are essential for negotiating the scree and crossing the river. Those daunted by the prospect of a 16km hike but eager to see the gorge have two options: either to do the first part of the walk, taking the breathtaking descent down the *xilóskala* ('wooden stairs'), with the disadvantage of the stiff climb back; or to start from Agía Rouméli, climbing 2km to get to the entrance, then continuing uphill into the gorge.

INFORMATION

- ✚ B2
- ✉ 43km south of Haniá
- ☎ 28210 67140
- 🕐 May–Oct, depending on weather, 6am–sunset
- 🍽 Tavernas (€€) at head of gorge and at Agía Rouméli; take refreshments for the gorge
- 🚌 From Haniá to the head of the gorge on the Omalós Plain. From Hóra Sfakión back to Haniá; check times locally
- ⛴ In summer 4–5 ferries a day from Agía Rouméli to Hóra Sfakión; daily afternoon ferry to Soúgia and Palaeóchora
- ℹ Head of the gorge
- ♿ None
- 👋 Expensive
- ❓ For details of walk ➤ 17

Górtys

🏠 D2

✉️ Agía Déka, Iráklio (46km south of Iráklio, 8km east of Moíres)

☎️ 28920 31144

🕐 Check for times

🍴 Cafés/bar (€)

♿ Few

💶 Moderate; free on Sun in winter

The ancient ruins, scattered among fields and hillsides, are eloquent evidence of the size and power of the former capital of Crete.

Not so ancient as the famous Minoan sites – in fact, rather insignificant in those days – Górtys came to prominence under the Dorians, ousted Phaestós from its pinnacle by the 3rd century BC and attained the ultimate status of capital of Crete after the Roman invasion of 67BC. Its tentacles of power reached as far away as North Africa, but in AD824 the great city was destroyed by the Saracen Arabs, and it has lain abandoned ever since.

Though the walls have crumbled and the columns have fallen, the extensive remains are a compelling evocation of the great city. The finely preserved apse of the 6th-century Basilica of Ágios Títos is built on the supposed site of martyrdom of St Titus, who was sent by St Paul to convert the islanders to Christianity. Nearby is the semi-circular Odeon, roofless now, but once a covered theatre where the Romans enjoyed musical concerts. And behind it, protected now by a modern brick arcade, are perhaps the most precious remains of the site – the huge stone blocks engraved with the famous law code of Górtys which, dating to 480–460BC, represents the first known code of law in Europe. In its archaic Dorian dialect, written from right to left on one line, then from left to right on the next, the code deals with civil issues such as divorce, adultery, inheritance and property rights, giving a fascinating insight into Dorian life on Crete.

The remnants of the acropolis lie on a hill to the west, and there are more remains along the road towards Agía Déka (but no parking there).

Plenty to see at the ancient site of Górtys

Haniá

On the north coast of the island the historic town of Haniá, which incorporates the island's most beautiful harbour, makes a delightful base.

The ancient city of Kydonía, inhabited since neolithic times, became the most important centre in Crete after the destruction of Knossós. The town fell into decline under the Arabs, but during the Venetian period (1204–1645) La Canea, as it was renamed, became 'the Venice of the East'. Following the Turkish occupation, which lasted from 1645–1898, Haniá was made capital of Crete and remained so until 1971.

Haniá is not only the best base for exploring western Crete, it is arguably the island's most appealing town. Beautifully set below the White Mountains, it has a lively harbour, a maze of alleys and a string of beaches nearby. Strolling is the most pleasurable activity, either along the harbour front, or through the streets of the old town, where Venetian and Turkish houses have been elegantly restored. Along the narrow alleys are such charming features as old portals and overhanging balconies, as well as enticing hole-in-the-wall craft shops and cafés.

The real magnet is the outer harbour, with its faded, shuttered houses, and its crescent of cafés and tavernas overlooking the water. This is where the locals come for their early evening *vólta*. The inner harbour, overlooked by Venetian arsenals, is another focal point, with fishing boats, pleasure craft and tavernas. Haniá may be picturesque, but there are often too many tourists crowding the narrow streets. To appreciate its beauty, try and visit early or later in the day.

INFORMATION

- B1
- Numerous cafés, tavernas and restaurants especially along the harbour (€–€€€)
- Regular services from outlying areas
- Odós Kriári 40, Mégaro Pántheon ☎ 28210 92943
- For a walking tour of Haniá ➤ 82

Down by the waterfront in Haniá

Iráklio

INFORMATION

➕ D2
🍴 Numerous cafés, tavernas and restaurants (€–€€€)
🚌 Regular services from outlying areas
ℹ️ Odós Ksanthoudídou 1
☎ 2810 246299

The fifth largest city in Greece, Iráklio is the capital of Crete and the commercial and cultural hub of the island. Busy and noisy it's still worth a visit.

This city was Herakleium to the Romans, Rabdh-el-Khandak (Castle of the Ditch) to the Saracens, Candia to the Venetians, Megélo Kástro (Great Fortress) to the Turks, it finally reverted to Herákleion (or Iráklio) in 1923. Badly damaged by bombs during World War II, it is today an essentially modern city.

Once a dusty town with an eastern flavour, Iráklio is now taking on a cosmopolitan air. Fashionable young people fill the cafés and smart boutiques sell the latest designs.

Everything of cultural interest lies conveniently within the ramparts and can easily be covered on foot. The most colourful quarter is the harbour, where fishermen gut their catch and skinny cats sniff around for titbits. Koúles Fortress overlooking the harbour and the nearby vaults of the arsenals are prominent reminders of the city's Venetian heyday. In the central Plateía Venizélos, cafés cluster around the fountain. From here the pedestrianised Odós Daidálos, lined with shops and tavernas, leads on to the huge Plateía Eleftherías and the famous Archaeological Museum (➤ 28).

Statue in front of Ágios Mínas Cathedral

Most of the architecture is postwar, but there are a number of old ruins or fountains, often incorporated into modern buildings and some neo-classical buildings. The Venetian walls, 40m thick in places, were constructed in 1462 on earlier Byzantine foundations, and extended in 1538. Most of the gates survive, and it is possible to walk along the line of the walls for about 4km, though only 1km of the walk is actually on top of the walls. Near here, is the tomb of Níkos Kazantzákis – Crete's most famous writer.

Istorikó Mouseío, Iráklio

Iráklio's history museum fills in all the gaps in Crete's powerful and turbulent past, plus an insight into Cretan art and culture.

This museum takes up the story where the Archaeological Museum (➤ 28) leaves off and provides a fascinating insight into the island's turbulent history, from the early Christian era to the 20th century. Slightly away from the city centre, the museum is free from the crowding that you find at the Archaeological Museum.

The collection starts with an exhibition of artefacts from the Christian period, with emphasis on the Venetian occupation and the Cretan War (1821–1898). This is illustrated by plans, photographs, explanations and a highly detailed model of Candia (Iráklio) in 1645. On the same floor the Ceramics Room illustrates the way in which pottery has evolved over 15 centuries.

The Medieval and Renaissance section displays Byzantine, Venetian and Turkish sculpture, Cretan-school icons, coins, jewellery and a collection of copies of Byzantine frescoes from Cretan churches. An early painting by El Greco (➤ 9) depicts a stormy *View of Mount Sinai* (*c*1570), with tiny figures of pilgrims climbing up the craggy peak to the Monastery of St Catherine.

The struggle for Cretan independence and the period of autonomy (1898–1913) is illustrated by portraits of revolutionaries, flags, weapons and photographs. The reconstructions of the studies of the writer Níkos Kazantzákis (➤ 9) and Emmanuel Tsouderós, Greek Prime Minister at the time of the Battle of Crete, bring you into the 20th century. The folk rooms on the fourth floor display local crafts and contain a replica of a traditional village home.

INFORMATION

🔲 D2
✉ Lysimáchou Kalokairinoú 7
☎ 2810 283219
🕐 Check for times
🍴 Waterfront restaurants nearby (€–€€)
♿ Only the first floor accessible for wheelchairs
💷 Moderate

Re-creation of a Cretan village room in the Historical Museum

Knossós

INFORMATION

➕ D2

✉ 5km south of Iráklio

☎ 2810 231940

🕐 Check for times

🍴 Café on the site (€€),
tavernas nearby

🚌 No 2 leaves from in front
of the Astória Capsís
Hotel, Plateía Eleftherías,
Iráklio, approximately
every 30 minutes

♿ Good (access as far as the
main court)

💷 Expensive

↔ Iráklio (➤ 36), Myrtiá
(➤ 60)

❓ Guided tours available in
four languages. Shop with
books and reproductions
of finds from Knossós

Famous fresco, Ladies in
Blue, *on display in the
museum at the Palace of
Knossós*

**The Minoan civilisation grew and
prospered around Knossós, the
largest and most powerful of the
palaces in Crete.**

A hundred years ago King Minos and Knossós
were merely names from the myths of ancient
Greece, but in 1894 British archaeologist Arthur
Evans purchased a site that transpired to be the
largest and most important palace in Crete and
gave credence to the myths. Excavations, which
began in 1900, revealed a 13,000sq m complex of
buildings, surrounded by a town of around 12,000
inhabitants. The elaborate rooms and the wealth
of treasures discovered were evidence of a highly
developed ancient civilisation, but it was the
labyrinthine layout and the sacred symbols on
walls and pillars that suggested Knossós as the
seat of the legendary King Minos and home of
the Minotaur. Hence Evans gave the name
'Minoan' to the newly discovered culture.

Knossós and other Minoan palaces on Crete
were founded around 1900BC but destroyed in
about 1700BC, probably by a series of
earthquakes. They were rebuilt but devastated
again in 1450BC, Knossós suffering least damage.
The final catastrophe came in about 1375BC and
Knossós was never rebuilt. The palace was more
than the residence of royalty – it was the seat of
administration and justice, an important
commercial centre and a centre of religious
ceremonies and rituals, with excavations
revealing chapels and shrines, sacred signs and
small statues representing goddesses.

Evans came under heavy criticism for
his restoration of Knossós, particularly for his
liberal use of concrete and his speculative
reconstructions and interpretations. But for the
casual visitor, it evokes the splendour of the
palace, and facilitates the interpretation of all
the Minoan sites.

Lassíthi Plateau

The Lassíthi Plateau is a dramatic geographical feature, whose flat, fertile fields are ringed by the towering peaks of the Díkti Mountains.

The most visited inland region of Lassíthi, the plateau has a spectacular setting, encircled by the Díkti peaks. Watered by the melting snow from the mountains, the soil is highly fertile, yielding potatoes, cereal crops, vegetables and fruit. Traditionally the land was irrigated by canvas-sailed windmills – the familiar symbols of Lassíthi – but these have gradually given way to the more efficient (if considerably less picturesque) diesel pumps. A few of the originals survive, and there is a row of ruined stone windmills at the Selí Ambélou Pass that heralds the plateau on its northern side. A circular road skirts the plateau (►19), passing through small villages with their simple tavernas and craft shops. To avoid the tour crowds at the Díkti Cave (►50), arrive very early in the morning or leave it until the early evening.

INFORMATION

🔠 E2
✉ Southwest of Ágios Nikólas
🍴 Tavérna Antónis (€) between the villages of Psichró and Pláti
☎ 28440 31581
🚌 Buses make a circular tour of the plateau, stopping at all villages
♿ No access possible to Díkti Cave, but villages can be visited
↔ Díkti Cave (►50)

Panoramic view of the Lassíthi Plateau from the entrance to the Díkti Cave

Moní Arkadíou

INFORMATION

✚ C1

✉ 24km southeast of Réthymno

☎ 28310 83116

🕐 Check for times

🍴 Snack bar (€) on the premises, taverna (€) at Amnátos (4km north)

🚌 4 buses a day from Réthymno

♿ Access to monastery only

💷 Inexpensive

The mass suicide within the Arkadíou Monastery came to symbolise Cretan heroism and strengthened the struggle against the Turkish yoke.

The fame of Moní Arkadíou lies not so much in its splendid setting on a plateau in the Ída Mountains, nor in its beautiful baroque façade, but in the historic role it played during the struggle for freedom from Turkish rule in the 19th century. Isolated in the mountains, the monastery became an important centre of Cretan resistance, supporting uprisings against foreign powers.

On 9 November 1866, following a two-day siege, thousands of Turkish troops forced entry through the western gateway. Within the monastery hundreds of resistance fighters were taking refuge with their wives and children. Rather than suffer death at the hands of the Turks, the Cretans blew themselves up, so the story is told, by setting light to the powder magazine. Most of the Cretans within the monastery were killed, but so were hundreds of Turks – the exact number of deaths is unknown. Following the event many prominent figures in Europe rallied to support the Cretan cause, among them Garibaldi and Victor Hugo. Nearly a century later the writer Níkos Kazantzákis (► 9) retold the historic event in his powerful novel, *Freedom and Death*.

Courtyard building at Moní Arkadíou

Visitors to the monastery can see the richly carved Venetian façade, dating from 1587, the restored interior of the church, the roofless powder magazine bearing scars of the explosion, and a small museum of icons, vessels and siege memorabilia. Close to the entrance to the monastery an ossuary containing the skulls of the siege victims is a chilling reminder of the events of 1866.

Moní Préveli

The peaceful setting overlooking the southern sea and the monastery's historic past combine to make Préveli one of Crete's most compelling sights.

When Crete fell to the Turks in the 17th century, the monks of Préveli decided to abandon their original monastery in favour of a more secluded location. Their new monastery, perched above the Libyan Sea, soon became a centre of resistance and grew wealthy on the olive groves, sheep, goats, wine, corn and other gifts that were bequeathed by Cretans who feared their possessions would otherwise fall into Turkish hands.

More recently the monastery sheltered Allied troops after the fall of Crete to the Germans in 1941, and assisted their evacuation from neighbouring beaches to the Egyptian port of Alexandria.

Largely rebuilt in 1835, then partially destroyed by the Germans in reprisal for the protection of the soldiers, the monastery retains none of its original buildings, but it is nevertheless a handsome complex with splendid views.

The finest feature is the Church of Ágios Ioánnis (St John), a 19th-century reconstruction of the original 17th-century church, containing an elaborate inconostasis with many old icons and a gold cross with diamonds, containing what is said to be a fragment of the True Cross. The story goes that the Germans tried three times to steal the cross but each time they tried to start their escape aircraft, the engines failed. A small museum within the church houses vestments, silverware, icons and votive offerings.

The church and remains of the original monastery, Káto Moní Préveli, can still be seen beside the Megapótomos River, 3km inland.

INFORMATION

- C2
- 13km east of Plakiás
- 28320 31246
- Check for times
- Snack bar (€) on premises in summer
- Limited bus service from Réthymno
- Boat trips to view coastal features, caves and grottoes
- Possible for wheelchairs
- Préveli Beach (► 57)

A time to reflect in the courtyard of the Préveli monastery

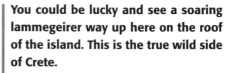

Óros Psiloreítis (Mount Psilorítis)

➕ C2
✉ 17km south of Anógia to base of mountain
🍴 None
♿ Not suitable

The snowcapped summit of Mount Psilorítis

You could be lucky and see a soaring lammegeirer way up here on the roof of the island. This is the true wild side of Crete.

At 2,456m, Mount Psilorítis, or Mount Ída, is the highest point on Crete. From Anógia a winding road through barren, mountainous terrain leads to the Nída Plateau at the foot of the mountain. Near the end of the road, by the taverna, a path leads up to the Idéon Ándron (Idéon Cave but also referred to as the Ída Cave), a contender, along with the Díkti Cave (➤ 50), for the title of birthplace of Zeus. Excavations in the 1880s yielded bronze shields from the 9th and 8th centuries BC, suggesting that the cave was a post-Minoan cult centre. Excavations in the 1880's yielded bronze shields, gold jewellery, hand drums, Minoan skeletons and many other objects generally dating from the 9th and 8th centuries BC suggesting that the cave with its altar was a post Minoan cult centre. You can walk down into the cave, but it is fairly shallow with no dramatic natural rock formations. The path to the summit of Mount Psilorítis also starts at the taverna – a gruelling 7–8 hour return trip.

Palaeóchora

Formerly a fishing village Palaeóchora has universal appeal, with its setting below the mountains, its excellent beaches and relaxed atmosphere.

This one-time haunt of hippies is still free from mass tourism. It sits on a small peninsula, crowned by the stone walls of a ruined Venetian castle built in 1282 and called Selínou; a name nowadays used for the whole region. Beneath it are two beautiful bays: to the east a sheltered but shingle and pebble beach, to the west a long stretch of wide golden sands shaded by tamarisk trees and popular with windsurfers.

Venizélos, the main street, is particularly lively at night, when the road is closed to traffic and taverna tables spill out on to the pavements. Despite its popularity the centre has not lost all its Cretan character – locals still frequent the cafés and fishermen land their catch at the quayside. With a population of 2,000 inhabitants, Palaeóchora is the most important town on the south western coast. Linked to coastal villages by a regular ferry service, the resort makes an excellent base for exploring southern Crete, and is well placed for hikers, with coastal and mountain walks. There are also weekend boats to the tiny island of Gávdos.

INFORMATION

➕ A2
✉ 80km southwest of Haniá
🍴 Tavernas along Venizélos (€–€€)
🚌 Regular service to Haniá
⛴ Ferries to Soúgia, Ágia Rouméli, Loutró, Hóra Sfakión and Gávdos
ℹ 028230 41507
♿ Few
↔ Soúgia (➤ 61)

Fishing is still an important part of life in the village of Palaeóchora

Pangía Kerá

INFORMATION

➕ E2

✉ Kritsá, 10km southwest of Ágios Nikólaos

☎ 28410 51806

🕓 Check for times

🍴 Cafés on premises (€), Paradise Restaurant across the road (€€)

🚌 Regular service from Ágios Nikólaos

♿ Few

💰 Moderate

↔ Kritsá (➤ 61)

❓ Icons and guides for sale at shop

This tiny church has beautifully restored Byzantine frescoes adorning its walls and domes that are remarkable for their realism and drama.

Set amid the olive and cypress trees of the Kritsá plain, this delightful little church dates back to the 13th and 14th centuries, and is a treasure house of religious art. Triangular buttresses supporting the aisles give the church an unusual appearance, but it is the interior, with the most complete series of Byzantine frescoes in Crete, that draws the crowds (arrive as early as possible to avoid the crush).

The only light in the church comes through the narrow apsidal windows and it takes time to decipher the different scenes. The very oldest frescoes are those of the apse, followed by the scenes from the Life of Christ in the dome and nave. More easily recognisable are the nave scenes of *The Nativity*, *Herod's Banquet* and *The Last Supper*.

Superb frescoes adorn the walls of the delightful church of Pangía Kerá

The later wall paintings of the south and north aisles show a marked move towards naturalism. In the south aisle (where you enter) the scenes from the life of St Anne and of the Virgin Mary are lively 14th-century frescoes, the faces full of expression. Note the face of Anne, whose portrait dominates the apse, and the touching scene in the aisle of Mary looking dejected over Joseph's misunderstood reaction to her conception. An angel descends to explain to Joseph. The north aisle frescoes portray scenes of *The Last Judgement*, depictions of St Anthony and other saints, and a portrait of the founder of the church with his wife and daughter.

Phaestós

Second only to Knossós in importance, Phaestós dominated the Mesará Plain, ruled by the legendary Rhadamanthys, brother of King Mínos.

The most striking feature of Phaestós is its dramatic setting, on a ridge overlooking the rich Mesará Plain. Excavations by an Italian archaeologist in the early 20th century revealed that the development of Phaestós followed that of Knossós: the original palace was built around 1900BC, destroyed in 1700BC and replaced by a grander palace. Unlike Knossós, however, this second palace (destroyed in 1450BC) incorporated foundations from the first palace. This makes interpretation somewhat confusing and time-consuming and there are no reconstructions (as at Knossós) to help, but the leaflet that comes with the admission ticket is quite useful.

Steps down from the entrance lead to the west court and theatre area via the upper court. The storage structures visible to the south of the west court were probably used for grain. The grand staircase leads up to the New Palace, with rooms overlooking the Old Palace (fenced off and still undergoing excavation). The huge paved central court, which has fine views of the Psiloreítis range of mountains, was originally bordered by a portico, foundations of which can still be seen. To the north the royal apartments (closed) were the most elaborate of the rooms, with the best views. It was in one of the chambers beyond these apartments, at the northern edge of the site, that the excavators discovered the famous Phaestós Disc, now in Iráklio's Archaeological Museum (➤ 28). Small, round and made of clay, the disc is inscribed with spiralling pictographics that to this day defy translation.

INFORMATION

- C3
- Phaestós , Iráklio (66km southwest of Iráklio, 8km west of Moíres
- 28920 42315
- Check for times
- Café (€) on the premises
- Regular services from Iráklio
- Tourist Pavilion on the premises
- None (lots of steps)
- Expensive
- Agía Triáda (➤ 25), Museum of Ethnology at Vóri (➤ 47)

The remarkable Disc of Phaestós

45

Réthymno

INFORMATION

➕ C2

🍴 Numerous cafés, tavernas and restaurants (€–€€€)

🚌 Regular services from outlying areas

ℹ️ Odós Elefthérios Venizélos (on the seafront east of the harbour)
☎ 28310 29148

The delightful historic town of Réthymno has a lovely harbour and sandy beaches that stretch to both sides of the town.

Réthymno was a town of little significance until the 16th and 17th centuries when it prospered under the Venetians. Following the fall of Constantinople, many Byzantine scholars sought refuge here and the town became an important intellectual and cultural centre. In 1645 it came under Ottoman rule, which lasted 253 years. The old quarter retains much of its Venetian and Turkish character and the town is still regarded as the 'intellectual capital' of the island.

The dominant feature of the town is the mighty Venetian fortress, built to defend the city against pirate attacks. To the east lies the harbour, where the waterside fish tavernas are a magnet for tourists. The narrow, pedestrianised alleys of the old town are ideal for strolling. Down virtually every street there are fascinating architectural details to admire, such as ornately carved Venetian doorways and arches, the Turkish overhanging wooden balconies and the minarets and domes which lend an exotic air to the skyline. Tiny shops are crammed with objets d'art, craftsmen sell leather or jewellery, grocery stores are stocked with herbs, spices and *rakí*. At the end of a morning's stroll head for the Rimondi Fountain, select from one of the surrounding al fresco cafés and tavernas and watch the world go by.

The Venetian lighthouse and boats in the harbour at Réthymno

The town has a wide sandy beach, backed by a palm-lined promenade and tavernas, hotels and cafés. The sands are packed in summer, but there are quieter beaches with cleaner waters away to the east and west.

Vóri

Vóri was put on the tourist map in 1985 when it became the home of the excellent Ethnologikó Mouseío Krítis (Museum of Cretan Ethnology).

A further boost came to the old village in 1992 with the award of Best European Museum by the Council of Europe. Inconspicuously located in a building near the church, it is a modern museum with exhibits beautifully laid out behind glass and informatively labelled. Devoted to traditional crafts and ways of life in rural Crete, the museum has separate sections dealing with food and diet, agriculture, weaving, pottery, metalwork, transportation and religion. The first section shows plants and other edibles with which Cretans used to supplement their meagre diets, and many of them are still used today, such as the group of wild plants called *hórta* and the aromatic plants for infusions.

The weaving section displays 25 different types of baskets made of reed, wild olive, rush, myrtle and other natural materials. The baskets served a variety of purposes, from trapping fish, harvesting sultana grapes and keeping snails to draining cheese. Pottery, made in Crete since Minoan times, includes vessels for *rakí*, vinegar and water, and storage pots for oil, wine, cereals and honey.

INFORMATION

- ➕ C2
- ✉ 4km north of Phaestós
- 🍴 Tavernas (€–€€)
- 🚌 Service from Iráklio

Museum of Cretan Ethnology
- ☎ 28920 91110
- 🕐 Check for times

Whitewashed house in the village of Vóri

Zákros Palace

INFORMATION

➕ F2
✉ Káto Zákros
☎ 28430 26897
🕐 Check for times
🍴 Akrogiáli (€), Káto Zákros beach ☎ 28430 26896
🚌 Twice a day in summer
♿ None
💰 Moderate; free on Sun in winter

Part of the appeal of the Minoan palace of Zákros is the remote valley setting by the coast, seemingly far removed from civilisation.

However, in Minoan times Zákros was a major centre, linked to a port (now submerged), trading with Egypt and the Middle East. The site was originally excavated by British archaeologists at the start of the 20th century. However they 'missed' the actual palace and it was not until 1962 that the Greek professor Nikólaos Pláton and the Greek Archaeological Society carried out more extensive diggings and discovered the palace and its archaeological treasures, their quantity and quality suggesting a highly affluent community.

The palace of Zákros covers an area of flat land on the floor of the river valley. The sea level has risen at this end of the island since Minoan times and the site is periodically waterlogged. The ruins are easily understood as compared to the other major sites as the palace itself is smaller and more self-contained. It dates from the New Palace period (1700–1400BC).

For an overall view of the setting and layout, start at the upper town; then climb down to the lower level and central court. From here, explore the ceremonial hall, a small banqueting hall and a cluster of other rooms, then cross to the royal apartments. The south side of the central court is bordered by workshops, and in the southeast corner excavators discovered 3,500-year-old olives preserved in water at the bottom of a jar. Treasures from the palace are housed in the Archaeological Museum at Iráklio (➤ 28) and Sitía's museum (➤ 60).

In the grounds of the palace of Zákros

CRETE's
best

Sacred Sites

ÁGIOS PÉTROS, IRÁKLIO

Just to the northeast of the Historical Museum of Crete, the evocative ruins and arches of Ágios Pétros lie between the sea and graffiti-splattered modern buildings. The church was built by Dominican monks in the first half of the 13th century and converted into the mosque of Sultan Ibrahim under the Turks. The southern chapel preserves the only 15th-century frescoes in Iráklio, but the church is currently undergoing restoration and is temporarily closed to the public.

➕ D2 ✉ Odós Sofokli Venizélou ☎ None ⏱ Currently closed to the public

ÁGIOS MÁRKOS, IRÁKLIO

The Basilica of St Mark, fronted by an arcaded portico, was built in 1239 by the Venetians and dedicated to their patron saint. The first church was destroyed by an earthquake in 1303 and its successor followed the same fate in 1508, but it was rebuilt and, like many others on Crete, became a mosque under the Turks. It later fell into decline but was restored in 1956–61 and today serves as an exhibition hall. Look out for the marble doorway inside, which is decorated with bunches of grapes.

➕ D2 ✉ Odós 25 Avgoústou ☎ 2810 399228 ⏱ Check for times 🍽 Cafés and restaurants (€–€€) nearby ♿ Few 💷 Free

DIKTAÍON ÁNTRO (DÍKTI CAVE)

According to myth, the Díkti Cave was the birthplace of Zeus. His father, Kronos, who feared being overthrown by a son, consumed the first five of his offspring. However, when Zeus was born, his mother Rhea presented Kronos with a stone instead of a baby and Zeus was concealed inside the cave, protected by warriors and fed by a goat. As a small child, he was then transferred to the Idéon Cave (➤ 42). The actual cave is impressive, but the site is highly commercialised and crowded. Beware of greedy car park attendants, costly donkey rides and persistent guides. Non-slippery shoes are essential. There are now concrete steps and lighting to help you negotiate the 65-m descent, but unless you are hiring a guide you may want to bring a torch to better examine the cave's natural features more closely. The cave is a kilometre up from the car park, via a steep, stepped path. An expensive donkey ride is the easy alternative. If you happen to arrive before the tour crowds, the dark cave, with its stalactites and stalagmites, is highly atmospheric. Down in the depths, the venue of ancient cult ceremonies, guides point out the chamber where Zeus was born, and features such as the face of Kronos and a stalagmite in the shape of Rhea and Zeus. Altars, idols and a large number of pottery and bronze votive offerings were found within the cave, some dating back to a pre-Minoan era.

Inside the Díkti Cave

➕ D2 ✉ Psychró, Lassíthi ☎ 29770 364335 ⏱ Check for times 🍽 Tavernas (€€) at the entrance, less commercialised ones in the village 🚌 Limited service from Iráklio and from Ágios Nikólaos ♿ None, highly unsuitable 💷 Expensive, particularly if you take a donkey and/or guide 🔁 Lassíthi Plateau (➤ 39)

MONÍ CHRYSOSKALÍTISSA

In a remote location at the southwest tip of the island, the whitewashed monastery perches on a promontory above the sea. It was founded in a cave in the 13th century, but the present building dates from the mid-19th century and contains little of interest to the average tourist. Of the 200 sisters who used to live here, just one and a monk remain. For centuries Moní Chrysoskalítissa, its barrel roof a distinctive landmark, was a refuge for victims of shipwrecks on this remote and treacherous coast. The name 'Chrysoskalítissa' means 'Golden Step', and was taken from the stairway of 90 steps leading from the nunnery down to the sea where, according to legend, one of the steps is made of pure gold – but is only recognisable to those who are free of sin!

🞤 A2 ✉ 13km southwest of Váthi ☎ 28220 61261 🕐 Check for times 🍴 Two tavernas (€) on the Váthi road 🚻 None 💵 Free 🔁 Elafonísi (➤ 29)

MONÍ TOPLOÚ

Square and solid, the monastery of Toploú lies isolated in the barren hills east of Sitía. Built in the 14th century, it was fortified to resist pirate attacks and named after a large cannon (*toploú* in Turkish) which was used against invaders. Today it is one of the richest monasteries in Crete. Geared to tourism, the complex may have lost some of its charm as a working monastery, but it certainly merits a visit, particularly for the icons and delightful cobbled courtyard overlooked by three tiers of monks' cells. The most notable of the many icons in the church is the remarkably detailed *Lord Thou Art Great* (1770), by Ionnis Kornaros. Beyond the church are engravings, icons and a display about the role which the monastery played against the Turks during the Cretan struggle for independence and during World War II.

🞤 F2 ✉ 16km east of Sitía ☎ 28430 61226 🕐 Check for times 🍴 Café/snack bar (€) 🚌 Bus service from Siteía then 3km walk from the main road 🚻 Few 💵 Moderate 🔁 Váï Beach (➤ 57)

SOÚDA BAY ALLIED WAR CEMETERY

Sheltered by the Akrotíri peninsula to the north, Soúda Bay is Crete's largest natural harbour. Laid out on a neatly tended lawn, sloping down to the water, are the graves of 1,497 Allied soldiers who died defending Crete in World War II. The names of the soldiers, many of whom lie in unknown graves, are listed in the Cemetery Register, which is kept in a box at the entrance to the building. Of the total Allied force on the island of 32,000 men, 18,000 were evacuated, 12,000 were taken prisoner and 2,000 were killed.

🞤 B1 ✉ 5km southeast of Haniá harbour ☎ None 🕐 All day every day 🍴 The tavernas in Haniá are more inviting than those of Soúda 🚌 Service from Haniá to Soúda Bay 🚻 Accessible to wheelchairs

TÉMENOS NERANTZÉ (NERANDZÉS MOSQUE), RÉTHYMNO

South of the Rimondi Fountain, the three-domed mosque's finest feature is its soaring minaret. Originally the Church of Santa Maria, it was converted into a mosque by the Turks shortly after their defeat of Réthymno. The minaret was added in 1890 and, prior to closure for safety reasons, afforded splendid views of the town. Today the mosque is a music school and concert hall.

🞤 C2 ✉ Odós Vernádou 28–30 ☎ 28310 23398 🕐 Closed to public except for concerts 🍴 Cafés and tavernas nearby (€–€€)

Sombre sights at the Soúda Bay War Cemetery

51

Museums

MODERN ART

The Centre of Contempary Art in Réthymno is also known as the L. Kanakákis Gallery. The stylish whitewashed galleries on two floors host temporary exhibitions of modern painting, sculpture and other media, mainly by Greek artists. It also has a collection of Greek art (only part of which is on view at any one time), including 70 paintings by Leftéris Kanakákis, a local artist.

🚼 C2 🖂 Odós Chimárras
☎ 28310 55847 🕐 Check
for times 🍴 In old town
(€–€€€) 🚻 None

ARCHAIOLOGIKÓ MOUSEÍO (ARCHAEOLOGICAL MUSEUM), HANIÁ

The Church of St Francis was the largest church to be built in Haniá during the Venetian era, and its spacious vaulted interior makes a handsome setting for the archaeological discoveries from excavations in the region. The exhibits span the period from late neolithic to Roman occupation, and greatly assist in adding a human dimension to the ancient sites of the area. The majority of artefacts date from the late Minoan era and include pottery, weapons, seals, decorated clay tombs (*larnakes*) and tablets inscribed with Linear A and B scripts. The Graeco-Roman section is represented by a collection of sculpture and glassware, leading up to three fine Roman mosaics, which were discovered in villas in Haniá, displayed at the far end of the church. The little garden beside the church features a damaged Lion of St Mark, and a beautifully preserved ten-sided Turkish fountain, dating from the period when the church was converted by the Turks into a mosque and the remains of the base for a minaret are still visible.

🚼 B1 🖂 Odós Hálidon 21
☎ 2821 90334 🕐 Check
for times 🍴 Cafés and
tavernas in Odós Hálidon or on
the harbour (€–€€€)
🚻 Accessible to wheelchairs
🚻 Moderate

A Minoan tomb inside Haniá's Archaeological Museum

ARCHAIOLOGIKÓ MOUSEÍO (ARCHAEOLOGICAL MUSEUM), RÉTHYMNO

Occupying the former Turkish prison at the entrance to the fortress, this is now a modern, well-organised museum of Minoan and Graeco-Roman finds from the Réthymno region. Especially noteworthy are the grave goods and decorated sarcophagi from the late Minoan period, some of them embellished with hunting scenes.

🚼 C2 🖂 Fortézza ☎ 28310 29975 🕐 Check for times
🍴 Centre of town (€–€€€) 🚻 None 🚻 Moderate 🔁 Centre of
Contemporary Art (➤ panel)

ISTORIKÓ KAI LAOGRAFIKÓ MOUSEÍO (HISTORICAL AND FOLK MUSEUM), RÉTHYMNO

The museum moved in 1995 from its previous site in Mesolongíou to the more spacious setting of a finely restored Venetian house, with a garden, near the Nerandzés Mosque (▶ panel 51). The galleries house a charming collection of crafts from local homes, including fine samples of embroidery, lace, basketware, pottery, knives and agricultural tools. Explanations, translated into English, accompany displays of bread-making techniques, Greek needlework and other traditional rural crafts.

✚ C2 ✉ Odós Vernádou ☎ 28310 23398 ⏰ Check for times
🍴 Cafés and tavernas nearby (€–€€) ♿ Few 🖐 Moderate

MOUSEÍO FISKÍS ISTORÍAS (NATURAL HISTORY MUSEUM), IRÁKLIO

Crete's wildlife, plants and landscape are attractively presented in this museum, set in a modern building outside the city walls on the road to Knossós. If you are planning a trip to the countryside or a drive around the island it will certainly enhance your appreciation of the things you will see. Life-sized dioramas on the ground floor re-create the island's flora and fauna in their natural habitats. Displays highlight birdlife and endangered species such as the Cretan wild goat, which can still be occasionally glimpsed in areas such as the Samariá Gorge. Glass cases in the gift shop house live snakes, the curious ocellated skink and the Cretan spiny mouse. The botanical garden is filled with aromatic wild herbs, while upstairs exhibits focus on the island's geological and human evolution.

✚ D2 ✉ Odós Knossoú 157 ☎ 2810 324711 ⏰ Check for times
🍴 Coffee shop on site (€) 🚌 2, 3, 4 from Iráklio 🖐 Free

NAFTIKÓ MOUSEÍO (NAVAL MUSEUM), HANIÁ

Tracing Crete's sea trade and maritime warfare, the Naval Museum is housed in the restored Venetian Firkás Tower guarding Haniá's harbour. Most of the exhibits here are models of ships, ranging from the simple craft of the Bronze Age (2800BC) to submarines built in the 1980s. The collection also contains marine weapons and instruments, historical documents, a model of the Venetian town of La Canea and, on the first floor, an exhibition devoted to the World War II Battle of Crete in 1941. Beyond the gate, the strategically sited bastion commands impressive views of the harbour, the lighthouse and the domed Mosque of the Janissaries (built in 1645, following the Turkish conquest). It was here, at the Firkás fortifications, that the Greek flag was first raised on Crete on 1st December 1913.

✚ B1 ✉ Fort Firkás, Aktí Kountourióti ☎ 28210 91875 ⏰ Check for times 🍴 Harbour restaurants (€–€€€) ♿ None 🖐 Moderate

The exterior of the excellent Naval Museum in Haniá

VIZANTINÓ MOUSEÍO HANÍON (BYZANTINE MUSEUM), HANIÁ

Haniá's newest museum is housed in a small, renovated church on the western side of the fortress. Byzantine artefacts include mosaics, sculptures and jewellery as well as the usual collection of icons. Oustanding are the brightly coloured fragments of 11th-century wall frescoes. The San Salvatore collection, in a brightly lit side gallery, includes a beautiful display of glass bead necklaces, jewellery, crosses, ceramics, Byzantine coins and a rare bronze lamp from the 6th and 7th centuries. There are also some fascinating post-Byzantine artefacts.

✚ B1 ✉ Odós Theotokopoúlou, 82 ☎ 28210 96046 ⏰ Check for times
🍴 Cafés and tavernas on the harbour (€–€€€)
♿ Accessible 🖐 Moderate

53

Historical Sites

FORTÉTZZA (VENETIAN FORTRESS), RÉTHYMNO

The Venetian fortress was built in 1573–1586 and is believed to be the largest Venetian fort ever built. It was designed to protect the entire population of the town. When the Turks attacked in 1645, the Venetian troops took cover here, along with several thousand townspeople; but following a siege of just 23 days, the fortress surrendered. Today the outer walls are well preserved, but most of the buildings were destroyed by earthquakes or by bombs in World War II. Inside the walls the dominant feature is a mosque built for the Turkish garrison and recently restored. Only ruins survive from the garrison quarters, the governor's residence, powder magazines and other buildings, but the atmosphere is very evocative and there are fine views of the town and coast. Plays and concerts take place here during the summer months.

➕ C2 ✉ Odós Kateháki ☎ 28310 28101 🕐 Check for times 🍽 Café (€) ♿ None 🚾 Moderate ↔ Archaeological Museum, Centre of Contemporary Art (➤ 52)

FRANGOKÁSTELLO

The great square fortress, formidable from a distance, is actually no more than a shell. It was built by the Venetians in 1340 in an attempt to subdue the rebellious Sfakiots and the pirates who were attacking Crete from the African coast. In 1770 the Sfakiot rebel leader, Daskaloyiánnis, was forced to surrender to the Turks here, and in 1828, during the Greek War of Independence, the Greek leader, Hadzí Micháli Daliáni, along with several hundred Cretans, died defending the fort against the Turks. According to the locals, on the anniversary of the massacre in mid-May their ghosts charge out of the castle on horseback across the sand dunes.

➕ B2 ✉ 17km east of Hóra Sfakión 🍽 Several tavernas (€–€€) 🚌 Limited service to Hóra Sfakión and Plakiás ♿ None 🚾 Free

LATÓ

The remains of this Dorian town (7th–3rd century BC) occupy a magnificent site, spread on a saddle between two peaks above the Kritsá plain. The layout of Lató is somewhat simpler than that of the Minoan sites and the extensive ruins, rising in tiers, are notable for the massive stone blocks used in their construction including the entrance gateway, the guard towers, the deep workshops with their wells, the olive presses and the corn-grinding querns. A stepped street with houses and workshops leads up to the central *agorá* with a shrine and a deep rainwater cistern.

➕ E2 ✉ 3.5km north of Kritsá, 10km west of Ágios Nikólaos 🕐 Check for times 🍽 Tavernas in Kritsá (€–€€) 🚌 Buses from Ágios Nikólaos to Kritsá ♿ None 🚾 Free

Walking to the ancient town of Lató

Minoan Sites

In the Top 25

2 AGÍA TRIÁDA (► 25)
13 GÓRTYS (► 34)
16 KNOSSÓS (► 38)
9 PHAESTÓS (► 45)
25 ZÁKROS PALACE (► 48)

GOURNIÁ

The ruins of the Minoan town of Gourniá sprawl over the hillside, just off the main Ágios Nikólaos–Sitía coastal road. The site is remarkably extensive, and the excavations revealed a thriving Minoan trading town of winding alleys lined by tiny houses, workshops, a marketplace and, on top of the hill, a palace. The palace was originally three storeys high, with pillars, courtyards, storerooms and apartments. In relation to Knossós and Phaestós this was something of a mini palace and its people more humble than in the other sites. Like the other Minoan sites of Crete, Gourniá was destroyed in 1450BC, then virtually abandoned. Many finds are housed in the Archaeological Museum in Iráklio (► 28) and a few in the museum at Sitía (► 60). If the site is closed, there is a good view from the lay-by next to the entrance track.

➕ E2 ✉ 19km southeast of Ágios Nikólaos ⏰ Check for times ☎ 28410 24943 🍴 Fish tavernas at Pachiá Ámmos (€–€€), 2km 🚌 Service to Ágios Nikólaos and Sitía ♿ None 💷 Moderate

MÁLIA

To the east of this resort lie the ancient Minoan remains of Mália Palace. The ruins are not as spectacular as those of Knossós, but the setting, on a quiet stretch of the coast between the sea and Lassíthi mountains, is rather more impressive. Those who have visited Knossós or Phaestós will recognise the layout around the central court, with store-rooms, ceremonial stairways, royal apartments and lustral basin. The origins are similar too. The palace was built in around 1900BC but destroyed by an earthquake in 1700BC. A second palace was built on the foundations, but (unlike Knossós) it was completely destroyed in the unknown catastrophe of 1450BC. Treasures from the site are now in the Archaeological Museum in Iráklio (► 28). French archaeologists are continuing to excavate a town which lay to the north and west of the palace. A 10-minute walk northeast towards the sea brings you to the Khrysólakkos (Pit of Gold), a burial site where priceless jewellery was discovered, which is now also in the Archaeological Museum.

➕ D2 ✉ 3km east of Mália ☎ 28970 31597 ⏰ Check for times 🍴 Café/bar on premises; restaurants (€–€€) in Mália (3km) 🚌 Regular service from Mália and Iráklio ♿ One of the few Minoan sites accessible by wheelchair 💷 Moderate

TÝLISOS

Reached off the old Iráklio/Réthymno national road, and set in the mountains, surrounded by olive groves and vineyards, Týlisos is home to three Minoan villas dating from the New Palace period (1700–1450BC). Like Knossós and Phaestós, which were built at the same time, there are signs of earlier structures. Excavated in the 20th century, the villas are referred to as Houses A, B and C, the best preserved being A (straight ahead as you enter the site) and C (the house on the left). The ruins are far less imposing than those of the famous Minoan palaces, but it is interesting to see where lesser mortals lived – it is also a delightful, peaceful spot for a stroll. House A, largest of the villas, has storerooms with reconstructed *píthoi* (large storage jars), a court with columns, a lustral basin and stairs which indicate an upper floor. House C is the most elaborate of the three.

➕ D2 ✉ 10km west of Iráklio ☎ 2810 831498 ⏰ Check for times 🍴 Taverna (€) next to the site 🚌 Service from Iráklio ♿ None 💷 Moderate

Ruins at Mália Palace

For Children

WHAT'S ON OFFER

The Cretans love children and welcome them with all the warmth and enthusiasm you would expect of a Mediterranean people. Apart from the water parks there are not many attractions that are specifically designed for children, but the island offers dozens of sandy beaches, sunshine for most of the year and sparkling blue waters for swimming and boat trips. For older children a wide variety of watersports facilities are available in all the main beach resorts and a number of discos, popular with teenagers.

BOAT TRIPS

Children enjoy the boat trip to the tiny island of Spinalónga (➤ 30) at the entrance to Eloúnda Bay. Some of the boat trips include swimming, and children can explore the island's fortress.
There are a number of boat trips from Réthymno's harbour that are sure to capture children's imagination. There are also daily sailings on two pirate ships to secluded unspoiled beaches. On board there are organised games. There are trips offering a chance to see dolphins along the south coast.

AQUA SPLASH WATER PARK

Close to Limín Hersónisou, Aqua Splash offers rides down huge tubes and chutes or more leisurely journeys in rubber rings down the 'Lazy River'.
➕ D2 ✉ Limín Hersónisou (on the road to Kastélli) ☎ 28970 24582 🕐 May–Oct daily 10–7

GEORGIOÚPOLI BOAT TRIPS

The Almirós river flows into the sea at Georgioúpoli and you can take paddle boats or canoes on the river to see the turtles (hopefully) and birds, including kingfishers.
➕ B2 ✉ Georgioúpoli Beach – the boats are next to the chapel on the causeway of the beach

LIMNOUPOLIS WATER PARK

This is the latest water park, in the west of the island, 8km south of Haniá. Facilities include a wide range of aquatic activities, restaurant, bar and shopping arcade.
➕ B1 ✉ Varípetro, Haniá ☎ 28210 33246 🕐 May–Oct daily, all day 🚌 Regular bus

LYCHNOSTÁTIS (CRETAN OPEN-AIR MUSEUM)

If your children are unmoved by Minoan remains and archaeological museums try the Lychnostátis 'living museum' of Cretan traditional life.
➕ D2 ✉ 1km from Limín Hersónisou ☎ 28970 23660 🚌 Service to Irákilo and Mália, bus stop 500m away

MUNICIPAL BEACH CLUB, ÁGIOS NIKÓLAOS

Beyond the bus station on the south side of the town, the main town beach of Ágios Nikólaos has a club with mini golf, children's pool, playground, gardens and snack bar. Instructions are given in watersports.
➕ E2 ✉ Municipal Beach, Ágios Nikólaos ☎ None 🕐 Daily 10–6. Closed winter

STAR WATER PARK

In Limín Hersónisou, this huge beach and pool complex offers waterslides and numerous watersports facilities as well as aerobics, mini golf, volleyball and a children's play area. Also sunbeds, hydromassage, cocktail bars and a choice of places to eat.
➕ D2 ✉ Beach Road, Limín Hersónisou ☎ 28970 24472/3 🕐 Apr–Oct daily 10–7 🚌 Regular service to Irákilo and Mália 🎫 Free entry; charge for individual attractions

WATER CITY

Crete's most popular water-based leisure park. The large complex has huge water slides, a wave pool and many other water-based activities. Bars, barbeuqe area, restaurants, shops and somewhere to change money.
➕ D2 ✉ Anópoli, Irákilo ☎ (2810) 781316 🕐 Apr–Sep daily 10–7 🚌 Service from Irákilo and Mália

Beaches

In the Top 25

7 **ELAFONÍSI (➤ 29)**
10 **FALÁSSARNA (➤ 31)**

FRANGOKÁSTELLO

Below the fortress (➤ 54) there is excellent swimming and snorkelling from the long sandy beach, and there are tavernas, shops, rooms to rent and even a disco. Less crowded beaches lie to the east and west.

B2 17km east of Hóra Sfakión Several tavernas (€–€€) Limited service to Hóra Sfakión and Plakiás

GEORGIOÚPOLI

The resort boasts a fine sandy beach stretching several kilometres to the east.

B2 22km west of Réthymno Tavernas on the main square (€–€€) Service to Réthymno and Haniá

MÁTALA

The beach at Mátala is beautiful but often crowded. The south-coast bay is famous for its rock caves (➤ 59), believed to early tombs .

C3 70km southwest of Iráklio Cafés and tavernas (€–€€) on the beach Services from Iráklio, Moíres and Phaestós Caves moderate

PRÉVELI

The beautiful sandy cove at the mouth of the Kourtaliótis Gorge can be reached by boat or by a steep and demanding walk from Moní Préveli (➤ 41). Idyllic off-season, the beach fills to overflowing with boatloads of tourists in the summer.

C2 38km south of Réthymno Two tavernas (€) Day trips from Plakiás and Agía Galíni

STAVRÓS

This near perfect scenic bay and beach, on the Akrotíri peninsula. (➤ 18), has clear shallow waters, perfect for children but does get busy.

B1 15km north of Haniá Two tavernas (€) Regular service from Haniá

VÁÏ

Backed by a plantation of rare date palms, the tropical-looking Váï beach lies at the northeastern tip of the island. The remote location is no deterrent and the lovely sandy bay is invariably crowded in summer. To see it at its best you must come early in the morning or off-season. The beach is strictly regulated, with a camping ban, car park charges and an extensive range of beach facilities.

F2 9km north of Palékastro Taverna (€€) on the beach Service to Palékastro and Sitía Good Car park charges

A view of the caves from the beach at Mátala

MÁLIA

The unashamedly brash and rowdy resort of Mália – along with neighbouring Limín Hersónisou – is the party capital of the island. Packed with discos, video bars and burger joints, it is similar to Limín Hersónisou, but has a far better beach, with sands stretching a considerable distance to the east.

GAIDOURONÍSI

Also known as Chrisí (the Golden Island) this is an unihabited island with idyllic sandy beaches, clear shallow waters and a small forest of cedar trees. It can be reached by excursion boat from Ierápetra.

BEACH SAFETY

Some beaches can have dangerous currents. Follow the flag warning signals and swim in the designated areas. Protect children from the hot Mediterranean sun with a high protection sunscreen – particularly between the hours of 11am and 3pm when the sun is at its hottest. Make sure children are also well protected when they are in the water.

Towns and Villages

The whitewashed chapel at the end of the causeway leading from Georgioúpoli

FÓDELE

Fódele is the birthplace of El Greco (➤ 9) – or at least it claims to be. Scholars now argue that the painter was born in Iráklio. But in any event the village makes a very pleasant detour from the main highway, along a verdant valley of orange and lemon groves. Along the main village road ladies sell linen, lace and embroidery and there are simple stalls selling citrus fruits. Over the bridge the village is less commercialised, with delightful streets lined by rustic, flower-decked dwellings. The El Greco House (Spíti El Greco) is well signed, and lies about 1km from the centre, opposite the Byzantine Church of the Panagía.

➕ C1 ✉ 19km northwest of Iráklio, 3km south of the E75 🍴 El Greco (€) 🚌 Two per day from Iráklio
Spíti El Greco ☎ 2810 521500 🕐 Tue–Sun 9–5 💷 Inexpensive

GEORGIOÚPOLI

This north coast resort was named in honour of Prince George, who became High Commissioner of Crete in 1898, after the Turks were forced to recognise the island's right to autonomy. The fishing village is now a well established resort, with hotels, rooms to rent and a huge sweep of beach. To explore the River Almyrós, its birdlife, crabs and turtles, you can hire pedaloes or canoes from the little chapel at the end of the causeway. The sandy beach stretches for several kilometres to the east where its shallow waters make it ideal for children. However, when the sea is rough, there are strong undercurrents that can make swimming dangerous.

➕ B2 ✉ 22km west of Réthymno 🍴 Tavernas on the main square (€–€€) 🚌 Service to Réthymno and Haniá 🚻 Few

KOLIMBÁRI AND MONÍ GONIÁS (GONÍA MONASTERY)

At the foot of the Rodopoú peninsula, Kolimbári is a pleasantly unspoilt coastal village, where local life goes on undisturbed by the few tourists who stay here. The beach is pebbly but the waters are crystal clear and there are splendid views over the Gulf of Haniá. About 1km north of the village the Moní Goniás has a delightful coastal setting. Founded in 1618, it has been rebuilt several times but the Venetian influence can still be seen in some of the architectural features. The small church contains some wonderfully detailed little icons from the 17th century along the top of the iconostatis, as well as votive offerings and other treasures. The most precious icons, dating from the 15th century, are housed in the museum, along with reliquaries and vestments. If the church and museum are closed, ask one of the monks to show you round. He will probably also point out the Turkish cannon ball lodged in the rear wall of the church.

➕ A1 ✉ 23km west of Haniá ☎ 28240 22281 ⏰ Monastery check for times 🍴 Seafront fish tavernas (€–€€) in Kolimbári 🚌 Service to Kolimbári from Haniá and Kastélli Kissámou ♿ Few 💰 Inexpensive

LOUTRÓ

The only way to get to this delightful, car-free village is on foot or by boat. It is a tiny, remote place, with white cubed houses squeezed between towering mountains and the Libyan sea. There are half a dozen tavernas, two hotels, rooms to rent and some villas, but the majority of visitors are daytrippers coming on ferries from Hóra Sfakión and Agía Rouméli. The pebble beach is not ideal but you can bathe from the rocks or hire canoes to explore offshore islets, coves and beaches. There are also boat trips to the sandy cove of Mármara and to Sweetwater Beach.

➕ B2 ✉ 5km west of Hóra Sfakíon 🍴 The Blue House (€) 🚢 Ferry service to Hóra Sfakíon and Agia Rouméli ♿ None

MAKRÝGIALOS

With one of the best beaches on Crete's southeast coast, the fishing village of Makrýgialos and its sister village Análipsi is a small but growing resort. Hotel development along the main road hides its charms, but head down to the waterfront for a delightful view of its curving sandy beach lined with pleasant tavernas. The gently shelving beach and warm shallow water is great for children.

➕ E2 ✉ 24km east of Ierápetra 🍴 Tavernas on the seafront (€–€€) 🚌 Service from Ierápetra and Sitía ♿ None

MÁTALA

Mátala made its name in the 1960s when foreign hippies (Cat Stevens and Bob Dylan among them) took advantage of the free accommodation offered by the historic rock caves. Unpopular with both locals and archaeologists, the hippies were thrown out long ago. Today Mátala attracts tourists of all ages, but it still appeals in particular to independent travellers – especially off-season. The climate is milder than the north coast and spectacular sunsets can be enjoyed from the beach tavernas and bars. Mátala's main attraction is its beautiful sand and shingle beach, sheltered between sloping ochre-coloured cliffs. Consisting of compacted, yellowy earth, the cliffs are riddled with man-made caves, particularly along the promontory on the north side. No-one knows who made the original caves, but they are generally believed to have been Roman or early Christian tombs. Behind the beach the village now caters almost entirely for tourists, but the resort is still pleasantly free of high-rise buildings.

➕ C3 ✉ 70km southwest of Iráklio ⏰ Caves 11.30–7 🍴 Cafés and tavernas (€–€€) on the beach 🚌 Services from Iráklio, Moíres and Phaestós 💰 Caves moderate

HÓRA SFAKIÓN

In the 16th century this was the largest town on the south coast, with a population of 3,000, but rebellions during the Turkish occupation left Hóra Sfakión largely impoverished, and what remained of the town was destroyed by bombs in World War II. Today it is no more than a small resort and ferry port, its main appeal the setting between the mountains and the crystal clear waters of the Libyan Sea. In high season the seaside tavernas of Hóra Sfakíon cater for boatloads of hungry hikers coming from the Samariá Gorge, waiting for buses back to Haniá.

➕ B2 ✉ 67km south of Haniá 🍴 Seafront tavernas (€–€€) 🚌 Service to Haniá and Plakiás 🚢 Ferries to Agía Rouméli (Samariá Gorge), Soúgia, Palaeóchora and the island of Gávdos.

MYRTIÁ

Myrtiá is a pretty place to visit, surrounded by vines and full of flowers and potted plants. It is proud of its Kazantzákis connection, and announces the museum at either end of the village in five languages. Níkos Kazantzákis' father lived on the central square in a large house which has been converted into a museum dedicated to the writer. Best known for his novel, *Zorba the Greek*, Kazantzákis was also a poet, travel journalist and essayist (➤ 9). The museum houses a collection of first editions of his books, costumes from his plays, stills from films of his books, photographs and personal belongings.

🔢 D2 ✉ 16km southeast of Iráklio 🍴 Cafés and tavernas (€) on the square. Níkos Kazantzákis Museum ☎ 2810 742451 🚻 Few 🎫 Moderate

NEÁPOLI

A pleasant provincial town and former capital of Lassíthi, Neápoli makes an obvious starting point for an excursion to the Lassíthi Plateau (➤ 39). Few tourists visit the town, but if you are passing by it is worth stopping at one of the cafés or tavernas in the main square to sample the speciality of the town, *soumádha*, a sweet drink made of almonds. A small museum on the square houses crafts and a handful of local archaeological finds.

🔢 E2 ✉ 21km northwest of Ágios Nikólaos 🍴 Tavernas in the main square (€) 🚻 None 🚌 Regular service from Iráklio and Ágios Nikólaos

PLAKIÁS

A rapidly expanding resort, Plakiás' main asset is its setting, with a long sweep of beach surrounded by steep mountains. It is a fairly low-key place with hotels and apartments, a couple of discos and several beach tavernas with lovely views of the sunset. The beach of shingle and coarse sand is rather exposed, but there's a better one at Damnóni, reached by car or a 30-minute walk.

🔢 C2 ✉ 22km southwest of Spili 🍴 Beach tavernas (€–€€) 🚌 Regular service to Réthymno 🚻 Few

A bird's eye view of the resort of Plakiás

SITÍA

The most easterly town in Crete, at the end of the national highway, Sitía feels quite remote. Both a working port and tourist resort, it is a pleasant, leisurely place, particularly around the taverna-lined quayside and the older streets above the harbour. The town dates back to Graeco-Roman times, possibly even as far back as the Minoan era, but it was under the Venetians that the port had its heyday. Today it is essentially modern, with buildings set in tiers on the hillside. The only evidence of Venetian occupation is the fortress above the bay, reduced to a shell by the Turks, but used now as an open-air theatre. Sitía's long sandy beach, popular with windsurfers, stretches east from the town, followed by the parallel coastal road.

The Archaiologikó Mouseío (Archaeological Museum), just out of the centre, has a good collection of Minoan works of art, with useful explanations in English. Particularly interesting is the section devoted to Zákros Palace (► 48), with decorated vessels, urns, cooking pots, a wine press and a collection of clay tablets with the rare Linear A script. In the entrance hall pride of place goes to the ivory statuette of a young man (*c*1450) discovered at Palékastro. The small Folk Museum, up from the harbour, has a collection of finely made traditional crafts, including baskets for carrying grapes, and bedspreads and rugs coloured with dye from indigenous plants.

➕ F2 ✉ 70km east of Ágios Nikólaos 🍴 Kástro (€€) 🚌 Services from Ágios Nikólaos, Iráklio and Ierápetra.
Archaeological Museum ✉ Odós Piskokéfalou 3 ☎ 28430 23917 🕒 Check for times ♿ Few 💰 Moderate
Folk Museum ✉ Odós Kapetán Sífi 28 ☎ 28430 22861 🕒 Check for times ♿ Ground floor only 💰 Inexpensive

SOÚGIA

Set against the backdrop of the Samariá hills, this former fishing port is rapidly expanding into a tourist resort. Remotely located at the end of a long twisting road from Haniá, it was first discovered by backpackers, but more and more tourists are coming for the long pebble beach, translucent blue waters, simple tavernas and coastal and mountain walks. As yet, accommodation is fairly basic. Just to the east of the Soúgia river mouth, a few Roman relics survive from the ancient port of Siía, which served the Graeco-Roman city of Élyros, 5km to the north. To the west a fine Byzantine mosaic, now in the Haniá Archaeological Museum (► 52), was discovered where the modern church stands. Three kilometres to the west of the village, reached by a local boat or on foot over the cliffs (70–90 minutes) lie the classical Greek and Roman ruins of the ancient city of Lissós.

➕ A2 ✉ 70km southwest of Haniá 🍴 Simple tavernas in the resort (€) 🚌 Service from Haniá ♿ None

VRÝSES

This busy village is located at the crossroads of the old Haniá to Réthymno road and the road which crosses the island from North (Georgioúpoli) to South (Hóra Sfakión). However the large modern church and enormous plain trees create an atmosphere of some tranquillity, where by the side of the dried up river bed you can eat local yoghurt and honey – delicious served with walnuts – at one of the many tavernas. Close by at Embrósnero is the tower of Ibrahim Alidákes, which is at present undergoing extensive restoration. The two beautifully frescoed Byzantine churches at Máza and Alíkambos, both painted by the famous artist Ioánnis Pagoménos, are also well worth a visit.

➕ B2 ✉ 46m southeast of Haniá 🍴 Tavernas by the bridge in the centre of the village; smaller cafés in the main street 🚌 Service from Haniá

KRITSÁ

Clinging to the slopes of the Díkti Mountains, Kritsá is a large hill village with fine views over the valley. Crafts are the speciality and shops are hung with rugs, embroidery and other homemade (and foreign) products. So close to Ágios Nikólaos and also home to the Panagía Kerá (► 44), this is a popular destination for tour coaches, but despite inevitable commercialism, the village retains much of its charm as a working hill community.

➕ E2 ✉ 10km southwest of Ágios Nikólaos 🍴 Tavernas (€–€€€) 🚌 Several a day from Ágios Nikólaos ♿ None

Crystal clear waters are the draw at the quiet resort of Soúgia

Places for Good Cretan Cuisine

CHEERS!

All restaurants serve Cretan wines, some also have a choice of other Greek varieties and a handful among the more formal restaurants have an international wine list. The dry Cretan bottled red and white wines go well with the oily food; the cheap house wine from the barrel, served in tin jugs, traditionally by the kilo, is often surprisingly good. After a meal you may well be offered a complimentary thimble full of *rakí*, perhaps accompanied by a tiny portion of baklavá or other sweet. All bars serve beer – locally-brewed Mythos, Amstel and Henninger or imported Heineken and Lowenbrau.

MEZÉDHES

These small plates of food make excellent starters or several can make a good main meal. Well-known dishes include the yoghurt and cucumber dip, *tzatzíki*, but there are many other, more adventurous, tastes to try.

Dine with a view over the Gulf of Merabéllo

CRETA HOUSE (€€)

Offers traditional Cretan cooking and some of the best *mezédhes* (➤ panel) in Sitía.
✉ Odós Konstantínou Karamanlí, Sitía ☎ 28430 25133

IPPÓKAMPOS (€€)

Overlooking the harbour, Ippókampos is famed for its *mezédhes* and is very popular with the locals, always a good recommendation.
✉ Close to the junction of Odós 25th August and Sófoklis Venizélou, Iráklio ☎ 2810 280240

LOUTRÓ (€)

Sifis is well-known for the quality of his meat and his delicious vegetarian dishes.
✉ On the old National road between Vríses and Fré
☎ 28250 71595

PÓRTES (€)

Nektários and Susana opened this quality restaurant in 2004. It is fast gaining a reputation as one of the finest eating places in town.
✉ Pórtou Street, Haniá ☎ 28210 76261

PYTHÁRI (€)

Excellent, family-run taverna with a shady terrace, perfect for a long lunch.
✉ Koutouloufári village, near Hersónisos ☎ 28970 21449

STELÍNA (€€)

Has a superb variety of Greek and vegetarian dishes. Closed on Mondays.
✉ Missíria (a suburb of Réthymno, 3km to the east)
☎ 28310 53192

TAVÉRNA ALÉXIS (€)

Aléxis and his family offer a friendly service and generous portions of tasty food.
✉ Just south of the main road, next to Ághios Nektários church, Mália
☎ 28970 32254

VÓTOMOS (€€)

A long established *psarotavérna* (fish taverna) with its own trout (*péstrofa*) farm. Very popular with locals and, of course, the fish could not be fresher!
✉ Next to the Ídhi hotel, Zarós ☎ 28940 31666

ZACHARÍAS TAVÉRNA (€)

Sitting in the welcome shade of mulberry trees, you can sample excellent Cretan food, with many organically-grown ingredients coming straight from Zacharías' own garden.
✉ Plátanos, on the road to Falássarna ☎ 28220 41285

CRETE
where to...

Iráklio

PRICES

Approximate prices for a full meal with a glass of wine:
€ = under €15
€€ = €15–€25
€€€ = over €25

TIME TO EAT

The opening times for restaurants vary greatly throughout the year. Usually in the summer months most places are open for lunch and dinner every day. However, some have a day off (often variable) and public holidays and religious festivals will also affect the programme. In the spring and autumn they will open for less days and even for less hours. Winter opening is much more restricted. Telephone numbers have been included in these listings where possible and it is advisable to call in advance, particularly if the restaurant is isolated and no easy alternative might be found in the immediate vicinity.

IONÍA (€€)

Slightly off the tourist track near the market, this restaurant dates from 1923 and is possibly the oldest on the island. Don't be put off by the non-descript decor. Locals come here regularly for the good selection of fresh Greek dishes. Try the snails with artichokes.
✉ Odós Evans 3 ☎ 2810 283213

IPPÓKAMPOS (€€)

Pleasantly placed overlooking the harbour, Ippókampos is famed for its *mezédhes* and is very popular with locals, which is always a good recommendation.
✉ Close to the junction of Odós 25th August and Sofoklís Venizélou ☎ 2810 280240

KÍRKOR (€)

The speciality of this café overlooking the Morozíni Fountain is *bougátsa*, the calorific, creamy custard pastry, liberally sprinkled with icing sugar.
✉ Plateía Venizélos ☎ 2810 284295

KYRIÁKOS (€€€)

When locals want to impress their guests, they take them to Kyriákos, long considered Iráklio's best restaurant. There is outdoor seating as well as a dining room, the formal atmosphere softened by lush plants and friendly service. Simple, but beautifully prepared dishes. It is essential to make a reservation in advance.
✉ Odós Dimokratías 51 ☎ 2810 224649

LA GRANDE TRATTORIA (€€–€€€)

Comparatively smart taverna with candlelit interior on two floors. Extensive menu, focusing on pastas, pizzas and Italian specialities with a creative, international flare.
✉ Odós Koraí 6 ☎ 2810 300225

LOÚKOULOS (€€€)

An elegant restaurant on one of Iráklio's prettiest streets, which lures fashionable young locals as well as tourists. The food is Mediterranean with the emphasis on pastas and pizzas. To complement your meal there are imaginative, very generous salads and delicious bread, baked in the wood oven.
✉ Odós Koraí 5 ☎ 2810 224435

TARTÚFFO (€–€€)

For those who want a change from Greek tavernas it is worth the 10-minute walk from the centre of town to this Italian restaurant. The distinctive wood-oven baked pizzas are particularly popular.
✉ Odós A. Papandréou 41 ☎ 2810 222103

TOÚ TERZÁKIS (€€)

This restaurant near the tiny church of Ágios Demetriós is popular with the local smart set for its initimate ambience. It features a familiar Greek menu but made using quality, organic ingredients.
✉ Odós Marinéli 17 ☎ 2810 221444

Iráklio & Lassíthi provinces

IRÁKLIO PROVINCE

ÁGII DÉKA

DIMÍTRIS TAVÉRNA (€)
Inviting roadside taverna
with tables in the garden.
Good homemade fare;
the speciality of charcoal-
grilled rabbit is particularly
recommended.
✉ Ágii Déka, near Górtys
☎ 28920 31560

KÁTO GOÚVES

MÝLOS TAVÉRNA (€€)
In a quiet, secluded back
street of Káto Goúves, this
attractive taverna provides
traditional fare, a good
choice of vegetarian
dishes as well as home-
made pizzas cooked in a
wood-fired oven.
Excellent home-made
wines and a genial
atmosphere lead to a
pleasant evening.
✉ South of the Pántheon Palace
Hotel ☎ 28970 42492

MÁLIA

TAVÉRNA ALÉXIS (€)
Aléxis and his family offer
very generous portions of
excellent food. The
service is efficient and
friendly.
✉ Just south of the main road,
next to Ághios Nektários church,
☎ 28970 32254

MÁTALA

**LIONS RESTAURANT
(€€)**
Although this is one of
several tavernas with an
inviting setting right on
Mátala beach, Lions'
menu is more varied than

most. Fresh seafoood
takes top billing, but
dishes like sole stuffed
with crabmeat have an
international flare. There
is also an upstairs open-
air bar for drinks and
snacks.
✉ Mátala ☎ 28920 45108

SKÁLA (€€)
You'll find this popular,
family-run taverna at the
far end of the waterfront,
set on top of the rocks
with wonderful views
across the beach. There's
fresh fish on the menu and
open-air dining on the
pretty terrace. A great
place to relax and unwind.
✉ Mátala ☎ 28920 45489

LASSÍTHI PROVINCE

ÁGIOS NIKÓLAOS

ÁOUAS TAVÉRNA (€€)
Not as overtly tourist-
orientated as the harbour
and lakeside restaurants,
and better value. Starters
range from octopus with
oregano to snails and fried
courgette balls. Follow
these with charcoal-grilled
meats or the daily
'special'. Attractive
trellised courtyard with
trees and potted plants.
✉ Odós Paleológou 44
☎ 28410 23231

ÍTANOS (€€)
Close to Plateía Venizélos,
up from the port, this
makes a welcome change
from the more
commercialised
restaurants around the
waterfront. Locals come
for genuine Cretan fare
and wine from the barrel.

STARTERS AND MAINS

If the starters look more varied
and appetising than the main
courses (as is often the case in
Greek tavernas), there is
nothing to stop you ordering
two of these and skipping the
main course altogether.

OLIVE OIL

Foreigners often complain
about the liberal use of olive
oil in the local cooking.
However, since the revelation
that Crete has the lowest rate
of heart disease and cancer in
Europe, more and more
tourists are showing an
interest in the local diet.

KAFENÍON

Every village on Crete has a *kafeníon*, the traditional Greek coffee-house where local men play *távli* (backgammon) or cards, discuss politics, exchange gossip and watch the world go by. The coffee they drink is known locally as Greek and elsewhere as Turkish – that is, thick, black and sweet, and served in tiny cups. If you don't have a sweet tooth ask for *skéto* (without sugar) or *métrio* (medium sweet). Due to tourist demand instant coffee is now also available in most cafés.

Tables on a terrace over the road.

✉ Odós Kyprou, 1 ☎ 28410 25340

LA CASA (€–€€)

This lakeside café/restaurant is as popular for its central location as for its simple fare, from spinach pies to *souvlaki* (meat cooked on a skewer).

✉ Odós 28 Oktovriou 31 ☎ 28410 26362

PÉLAGOS (€€€)

Save this for a special occasion. It is Agíos Nikólaos' smartest taverna, set in a neo-classical building with a large courtyard shaded by palms. The emphasis is on fish and seafood.

✉ Odós KatehÁki 10 ☎ 28410 25737

ELOÚNDA

FERRYMAN TAVERNA (€€)

This waterside restaurant takes its name from the old BBC television series, *Who Pays the Ferryman?*, which was filmed at nearby locations. The Cretan menu is a cut above the usual fare, with more elaborate dishes such as pork cooked with bacon, mushrooms and garlic in a wine sauce. Try rusk-like Cretan bread.

✉ On the waterfront ☎ 28410 41230

IERÁPETRA

NAPOLEON THE GREAT (€€)

Opposite the waterfront and handy for the town centre, this is one of the oldest and long-established restaurants in town. Specialising in fresh fish and traditional bakes, it is a favourite with both locals and tourists alike.

✉ Odós Stratigóu Samouél 26 ☎ 28420 22410

KÁTO ZÁKROS

AKROGIÁLI (€€)

In a friendly atmosphere and a beach-side setting on the east coast, Níkos Perákis deserves his long-standing reputation for his local fresh fish and meat.

✉ On the waterfront ☎ 28430 26896

KOUTOULOUFÁRI

PYTHÁRI (€)

Excellent, family taverna with a shady terrace, high up in the hills overlooking Hersónisos.

✉ Koutouloufári village, near Hersónisos ☎ 28970 21449

MAKRÝGIALÓS

KÁVOS (€€)

The fresh seafood and homemade Cretan specialities change daily at this taverna by the waterfront. It has its own bakery, and the excellent wine comes from the grandfather's vineyard in a nearby village.

✉ On the waterfront ☎ 28430 51325

MARIDÁTIS

TAVÉRNA MARIDÁTIS (€)

Manólis and his partner Níki prepare fresh fish, meat and traditional

mezédhes in this popular taverna closee to the beach.
✉ 5km from Palékastro, on the road to Vái ☎ No phone

MOCHLÓS

RESTAURANT KAVOÚRIA (€€)
This waterside taverna overlooks a sandy cove, its bright blue and green wooden tables and chairs matching the colours of the ocean. A good range of Greek dishes and fresh fish complement the beautiful views.
✉ On the waterfront
☎ 28430 94204

PALÉKASTRO

RESTAURANT ÉLENA (€)
Next to the tourist office, this is a taverna of great character, offering Cretan specialities such as rabbit cooked in wine, *briam* (aubergines and courgettes), cheese pies and stuffed vine leaves. Wine comes from the barrel and there are home-made sweets and ice creams.
✉ Opposite the chemist, Palékastro ☎ 28430 61234

SITÍA

CRETA HOUSE (€€)
The large outdoor terrace is set right along the waterfront near the beach. The indoor restaurant is charmingly decorated with a re-creation of a Cretan house. It serves good Greek and Cretan specialities and fresh fish.
✉ Odós Karamanli 10
☎ 28430 25133

MÍXOS (€€)
Set back from the harbour, this is where you'll find the locals dining out. Plenty of good-value Cretan dishes and charcoal-grilled fish and meat, with heady wine from the barrel to complement the food.
✉ Odós Vinzétzos Kornárou 117
☎ 28430 22416

TZERMIÁDO

KRÓNIO (€)
This is the oldest restaurant on Lassíthi Plateau, established before the advent of tourism. Authentic Greek fare includes *stifado*, which is made fresh daily, lamb with white artichokes (spring only), *dolmades* and cuttle fish with spices. All dishes use fresh local produce. Delicious cheese and vegetable pies are served as starters or as a snack. The charming Vassilis and his French wife, Christine, encourage customers to take a good look in the kitchen before making their choice. The best time to do so is around noon.
✉ Lassíthi Plateau ☎ 28440 22375

ZARÓS

VÓTAMOS (€€)
A long-established *psarotavérna* (fish taverna) with its own trout (*péstrofa*) farm. Very popular with locals, and of course the fish could not be fresher!
✉ Next to the Ídhi hotel, Zarós
☎ 28940 31666

TIRÓPITTA
A favourite snack among the Cretans are *tirópitta*, delicious hot pastries filled with feta cheese. Other readily available snacks are *souvlaki* (chunks of meat on a skewer), sweet pastries or salted nuts, pumpkin seeds and chick peas, sold from street carts.

Haniá

TAVERNAS AND RESTAURANTS

Eating establishments are normally called tavernas or *estiatória* (restaurants) and the difference between them is not very clear cut. These days tavernas range from no-frills family-run places with plastic tablecloths to smarter establishments catering primarily for tourists. *Estiatória* are traditional restaurants serving local dishes, usually more upmarket and expensive than tavernas and often with lovely surroundings. Meat-eaters will enjoy the *psistariá*, where chicken, lamb, pork, kebabs and other meats are barbecued over charcoal.

HANIÁ TOWN

APOSTÓLIS (€€)

A good quality *psarotavérna* (fish taverna) with a delightful harbour-side setting overlooking the fishing boats. Very popular with locals and tourists alike.

✉ Aktí Enóseos 3 ☎ 28210 41767

BOUGÁTSA IORDÁNIS (€)

Bougátsa, a pie made from fílo pastry filled with fresh *myzíthra* cream cheese and served hot, with a sprinkling of sugar, is a speciality of Haniá that should not be missed. Iordannis' father-in-law bought the bakery from a Muslim, who taught him the recipe in 1924 and since then the tradition has continued. Note that these bakeries are only open in the mornings when you can stock up for your picnic.

✉ Apokorónou 24 and Kydonías 96 ☎ 28210 88855/90026

ÉLA (€€)

This atmospheric restaurant is set inside the ochre walls of a roofless Venetian building. The Cretan cuisine includes wonderful lamb and chicken dishes, steaks, fresh fish and vegetarian dishes such as *boureki*. There's a good range of wines and live music too.

✉ Odós Kondiláki 47 ☎ 28210 74128

KARIÁTIS (€€–€€€)

Located behind the former customs house, this unique, upmarket

Italian restaurant enjoys a good reputation for its pastas, pizzas and fresh salads. It also has an extensive choice of wines.

✉ Plateía Kateháki 12 ☎ 28210 55600

MICHÁLIS (€€–€€€)

Superbly situated on the old harbour, overlooking the lighthouse, Michális has established a sound reputation based on his choice of fresh local produce and recipes from Haniá.

✉ Aktí Tombázi/Sourméli 54–56 ☎ 28210 58330

NIKTERÍDA (€€€)

On the neck of the Akrotíri peninsula, a short taxi ride from Haniá. A restaurant recommended by locals in the know, serving well prepared Cretan and other Mediterranean food. Garden with wonderful views across Soúda Bay. Good selection of wines. Occasionally there is traditional music, which is why it is used by tour companies as part of their Cretan evenings.

✉ Korakiés ☎ 28210 64215

PÓRTES (€€)

Nektários and Susana opened this quality restaurant in a narrow back street behind the harbour in 2004 and it has quickly gained a reputation as one of the finest eating places in town.

✉ Odós Pórtou 48 ☎ 28210 76261

SUKI YAKI (€€)

Good Chinese and Thai cooking in a stylish

restaurant next to the Archaeological Museum. The courtyard, where tables are laid in summer, overlooks the museum garden with its Turkish fountain.

✉ Hálidon 28
☎ 28210 74264

TAMÁM (€€)

Converted from a part of the old Turkish baths, and serving Greek, Cretan, Turkish and Arabic specialities, this is one of Haniá's most popular haunts. The interior, which is below street level, has fairly basic decor but is candlelit and full of atmosphere. In summer the tables pack the pavement outside. The house wine is served in a jug straight from the barrel.

✉ Odós Zambelíou 49
☎ 28210 96080

THALASSINÓ AGÉRI (€€)

A charming fish restaurant just to the east of the old town in the area known as Tabakariá. With tables and chairs placed literally a few feet from the sea and surrounded by the old tannery buildings the setting is unique. You can be promised some wonderful sunsets from this restaurant.

✉ Vivláki 35, Tabakariá
☎ 28210 51136/56672

THÓLOS (€€€)

The evocative setting, within the ruins of a Venetian town house, combined with the quality of the Cretan meat dishes, makes this one of Haniá's most desirable tavernas.

✉ Ágion Déka 36 ☎ 28210 46725

TO PIGÁDI TOÚ TOÚRKOU (WELL OF THE TURK) (€€€)

As the name suggests, this cellar restaurant has an eastern flavour, with spicy food and atmospheric Arabic music.

✉ Kalinikou Sarpáki 1–3, Splántzia ☎ 28210 54547

HANIÁ PROVINCE

FRÉ

LOUTRÓ (€–€€)

Sífis is well-known for the quality of his meat and his delicious vegetarian dishes, all served in a delightful, refreshing setting amongst the trees.

✉ On the old National road between Vríses and Fré
☎ 28250 71595

KASTÉLLI KISSÁMOU

TO KELÁRI (THE CELLAR) (€€)

On the beachfront promenade, overlooking the beautiful bay of Kíssamos, Stélios takes justifiable pride in his local cuisine.

✉ Beachfront, Kastélli Kissámou
☎ 28220 23883

PAPADÁKIS (€)

On the seafront, this is probably the best value taverna in Kastélli Kissámou for fresh fish. Lobsters, sword fish, shrimps and baby squid are likely to be on the menu.

✉ Plateía Telonio
☎ 28220 22340

RAKÍ

Be prepared for a complimentary glass of *rakí* (or *tsikoudiá*) at the end of your meal. This ubiquitous spirit, drunk neat in small glasses, is distilled from the skin and pips of grapes. Many Cretans drink it daily, and in winter it is taken with honey to provide relief from colds.

Haniá & Réthymno

GREEK CHEESES

Crete has a variety of cheeses, including the ubiquitous feta, a white semi-soft salted cheese served with *horiátiki* (Greek salad), the Cretan *myzíthra*, a ewe's milk cheese similar to ricotta, which comes either sweet or salted, and *graviéra*, a hard, sharp, yellow cheese.

LOUTRÓ

THE BLUE HOUSE (€)
The combination of the views over Loutró's harbour, the excellence of the seafood and Greek cuisine and the friendly atmosphere make this one of the most inviting restaurants on Haniá's southern coastline. The only access is by foot or ferry (► 59). The Blue House is also a guest house, but Loutró is a very popular little port and you would be lucky to find a room available in season without booking well in advance. A perfect Cretan experience.
✉ Loutró ☎ 28250 91127

PALAEÓCHORA

DIÓNYSOS (€€)
One of many tavernas along the main street of this busy south coast resort, with tables spilling out on to the pavement. You can make your selection of the dishes from the kitchen in true Greek style.
✉ Vénizelos
☎ 28230 41243

PLÁKA

HAROKÓPOS (€)
Pleasantly situated in the village square in Pláka, which is located above the beach resort of Almerída, this traditional taverna offers excellent home-cooking served up in generous portions. Good local house wine and friendly owners.
✉ Pláka Apokorónou
☎ 28250 32089

PLATANIÁS

MÝLOS (€€€)
This popular taverna not only serves some of the best Cretan food in the area (particularly the excellent range of charcoal grilled meats) but also has a delightful garden setting with a watermill and duck pond. A lovely spot for a leisurely lunch treat.
✉ Plataniás, 12km west of Haniá ☎ 28210 68578

PLÁTANOS

ZACHARÍAS TAVERNA (€)
You can sample excellent Cretan food, with many organically-grown ingredients coming straight from Zacharías' own garden, under the welcome shade of mulberry trees.
✉ Plátanos village, on the road to Falássarna ☎ 28220 41285

RÉTHYMNO TOWN

AVLÍ (€€€)
Splash out for a meal in this elegant restaurant within an old Venetian manor house. Good wine list. There's a delightful courtyard for outdoor meals. Book in advance.
✉ Odós Xanthoudídou 22
☎ 28310 26213

GLOBE (YDRÓGEIOS) (€€)
A good restaurant/snack bar situated opposite the beachfront promenade. Cretan specialities, pasta dishes, pizzas, crepes, coffees, ice creams and much more are prepared by the owner and chef, Ágis. Choices for vegetarians.

✉ El. Venizélou 33
☎ 28310 25465

KYRIÁ MARIA (€)

Customers choose their dishes from the kitchen where everything is home-made: *pastitsio*, lamb in lemon sauce, pork and rabbit and a good choice of vegetable dishes. Before ordering dessert it is worth bearing in mind that after your meal, cheese pies and honey are on the house.
✉ Odós Moshovítou 20
☎ 28310 29078

ÓTHONAS (€–€€)

Overtly touristy, in the centre of the old town, but a great spot for people-watching. Steaks, pasta dishes and home-made sauces are the specialities, but there are numerous other international dishes to choose from. Lively, bustling atmosphere. Set menus available.
✉ Plateía Plátanos 27
☎ 28310 55500

ZAMBÍA (€)

An especially good restaurant for lunch with many fish and traditional Greek dishes. Go into the kitchen and see what they have to offer, as there are seasonal variations.
✉ Odós Stamathioudháki 20, Koumbés (close to the municipal swimming pool) ☎ 28310 24561

RÉTHYMNO PROVINCE

AGÍA GALÍNI

ÓNAR (€€)

The main attraction here is the splendid harbour and sea views from the roof garden restaurant. Wide range of Greek dishes, as well as home-made pizzas, pasta, fresh fish. The restaurant is expanding to take over the ground floor.
✉ Agía Galíni ☎ 28320 91288

ARGIROÚPOLIS

PALAIÓS MÍLOS (AU VIEUX MOULIN – THE OLD MILL) (€€)

Yiórgos and Sýlvia run this restaurant, stunningly set among the springs of what was once ancient Lappa. Grilled meats are the speciality.
✉ Argiroúpolis
☎ 28310 81209

MISSÍRIA

STELÍNA (€€)

Vangelió and Níkos have a truly superb variety of appetising Greek and vegetarian dishes, some of them unique to their establishment.
✉ Missíria (a suburb of Réthymno, 3km to the east of the old National road) ☎ 28310 53192

ZÍSIS (€–€€)

An excellent choice for lunch and much frequented by the locals, especially on Sundays when it is packed. Zísis boasts a vast array of freshly cooked food in baking trays & casseroles – just go inside and make your choice.
✉ Máhis Krítis 63-65 (4km east of Réthymno on the old National road) ☎ 28310 28814

DINING AL FRESCO

Greeks dine late (from 9pm) and enjoy sitting outside to eat – either on a street pavement, a taverna courtyard or a seaview terrace.

EXTRAS

A service charge of 15 per cent is usually included in your bill. If you are particularly pleased with the service you can leave a little extra for the waiter.

Iráklio

PRICES

Approximate price for a double room for one night. (Prices are for the room, not per person.)

€ = under €50
€€ = €50–€100
€€€ = over €100

RENTING ROOMS

All over Crete you will see signs for 'Rent Rooms'. These are graded from A to C and could be in an uninspiring modern block or a friendly private home. Accommodation in the latter is often more pleasant and a good deal cheaper than a room in a low category hotel. Discounts are normally given on stays of three nights or more.

IRÁKLIO TOWN

ASTÓRIA CAPSÍS HOTEL (€€€)

Modern hotel close to the Archaeological Museum on the busy Eleftherías Square in the centre of Iráklio Town. There is some noise from the busy streets around the hotel, but it makes up for this with good facilities including a fourth-floor swimming pool with snack bar, main restaurant and ground floor Café Capsís. There are 14 suites and 117 air-conditioned rooms.
✉ Plateia Eleftherías ☎ 2810 343080; fax: 2810 229078

EL GRECO (€€)

On a busy shopping street, this is one of the town's most central hotels. There are 90 adequate rooms. The public rooms include a cafeteria and breakfast room. Can be noisy.
✉ 4 Odós 1821
☎ 2810 281071; fax: 2810 281702

KRÓNOS HOTEL (€€)

The appearance of this modern block may be uninspiring, but don't be deceived, this is a friendly, family-run place with an excellent location, right on the seafront and with several tavernas nearby. Most rooms have sea view. Open all year.
✉ Sofoklis Venizélou 2
☎ 2810 282240; fax: 2810 285853

LATÓ (€€)

A stylish, well-equipped hotel, close to the old port and the museum, the Lató caters for both business and pleasure. Modern, soundproofed guest rooms come with TV, air conditioning, Internet access, minibars and balcony; some overlook the fortress by the port. Book in advance as it is popular.
✉ Epimenídou 15 ☎ 2810 228103; fax: 2810 240350

AGÍA PELAGÍA

SOFITÉL CAPSÍS PALACE & BUNGALOWS (€€€)

One of Crete's largest and most luxurious complexes, set on a peninsula with sandy bays either side. The hotel comprises two main buildings and villa-like bungalows set among beautifully maintained gardens. Facilities include two sandy beaches, indoor and outdoor pools, watersports, fitness centre, shopping arcade, and even a zoo which includes the rare Cretan ibex. The Tavérna Poseidón offers 30 different Greek *mezédhes*, fresh local fish, music and wonderful views across the bay.
✉ Agía Pelagía ☎ 2810 811212; fax: 2810 811076
🚌 Regular service to Iráklio

MÁTALA

HOTEL ZAFÍRA (€€)

Mátala's largest hotel has 70 rooms and is on the main road in the town centre. Rooms are simple, but all have a balcony facing either the sea or the hills inland. There is a hotel bar and restaurant.
✉ Mátala ☎ 2810 45112; fax: 2810 45725

Lassíthi

ÁGIÓS NIKÓLAOS

MÍNOS BEACH (€€€)

Before the Eloúnda Beach was built this hotel enjoyed a reputation as the finest hotel on the island. Lying on a secluded promontory near the centre, it provides luxurious accommodation in the main block or bungalows, a good choice of watersports and swimming from rocky inlets, sandy beaches or the hotel's heated outdoor pool. The equally luxurious Minos Palace nearby is owned by the same company.

✉ Ágios Nikólaos 72100
☎ 28410 22345; fax: 28410 22548

ELOÚNDA

ELOÚNDA BEACH HOTEL (€€€)

A member of the Leading Hotels of the World group, this is generally recognised as the most exclusive resort hotel in Greece. The roll call of VIP guests includes prime ministers and presidents. The luxurious rooms, bungalows and suites have bay or garden views. Italian, Greek and international restaurantss a private sandy beach, heated outdoor pool, health and fitness centre, floodlit tennis courts, watersports centre and limousine and heli-pad. Also in this hotel group located in this area is the Eloúnda Bay Palace.

✉ 72 053 Eloúnda ☎ 28410 41412/3; fax: 28410 41373; www.lhw.com

KALÓ HORIÓ

ELPÍDA HOTEL (€€)

Well away from the bustle of Ágios Nikólaos, the hotel is set on a peaceful hillside overlooking sea and mountains. The two beaches of Kaló Horió are the best in the area – alternatively you can use the open-air pool. The hotel has a restaurant, lounge/bar, pool snack-bar, and children's playground.

✉ Kaló Horió, Merabéllo
☎ 28410 61403; fax: 28410 61481

ÍSTRON BAY HOTEL (€€€)

This secluded hotel, 13km east of Ágios Nikólaos, has a cliff-hanging setting above a glorious small bay. There are 145 sea-view rooms in local style, three restaurants (the hotel is well-known for its cuisine), open-air pool, tennis, beach bar, watersports, fishing trips and organised day and evening activities.

✉ Kaló Horió ☎ 28410 61303; fax: 28410 61383
🚌 Regular service to Ágios Nikólaos, Iráklio and Sitía

PALÉKASTRO

HOTEL HELLÁS (€)

This modest and very inexpensive family-run hotel lies in the centre of the village. Rooms come with air-conditioning and balconies. The restaurant/café, with good-value food, is popular with locals.

✉ Palékastro ☎ 28430 61240 🚌 Services to Sitía, Vái and Káto Zákros

HOT AND COLD

Don't be surprised if hot water is in short supply. Many properties in Greece have solar-powered heating systems and cloudy weather may mean short supplies. Some places may have a back-up electrical system to cover for bad weather.

Haniá

PRICES

Hotel prices, which vary according to the season, are strictly controlled by the government. Off-season there are normally substantial discounts on the official rates. In high season, however, you may be hit by hidden extras such as surcharges for air conditioning or a stay of less than three nights.

HANIÁ TOWN

AMPHORÁ (€€)

A prime location on the Venetian harbour and beautifully renovated rooms within a historic house make this one of the most desirable central hotels of Haniá. The building is partly Venetian, partly Turkish and every room is different. Breakfasts of various breads, cheeses, ham, fruit and home-made jams.The hotel has the addeed bonus of a harbourside restaurant.
✉ Párados Theotokopoúlou 20 ☎ 28210 93224; fax: 28210 93226

CONTÉSSA (€€)

On a narrow street in the Venetian quarter, with views of the harbour, this is a charming old-fashioned guest house. There are only six bedrooms, and you would need to book in advance for the high season.
✉ Theofánous 15 ☎ 28210 98566 (also fax)

DOGE APARTMENTS (€€)

This old Venetian house, just up the street from the port, has been converted into eight fully equipped apartments for two to five people.
✉ Odós Kondilaki 14–16 ☎ 28210 95466; fax: 28210 96020

HALÉPA (€€)

Located in the elegant quarter of Halépa, the house was built in the 19th century and was formerly used as the British Embassy. It has 46 air-conditioned rooms (many with sea views), a dining room, palm-tree garden and relaxing sun terrace.
✉ Elefthérios Venizélos 164 ☎ 28210 28440; fax: 28210 28439 🚌 Regular service to central Haniá

NÓSTOS (€€)

Delightful bed-and-breakfast in a converted Venetian house on one of Haniá's prettiest alleys. Some rooms have sea views.
✉ Zambelíou 42-46 ☎ 28210 94743; fax: 28210 94740

PÓRTO VENEZIÁNO (€€)

A modern, comfortable, 'Best Western' hotel, with spacious rooms (many with sea views), TV & air-conditioning, reception area, dining room and a coffee bar with tables on the quay side. Extremely pleasantly situated by the fishing boats and the marina and just a short walk from the town centre.
✉ Ákti Enóseos, Old Venetian Harbour ☎ 28210 27100; fax: 28210 27105

LOUTRÓ

PORTO LOUTRÓ (€€)

The only way you can get to this charming little hotel, set on Loutró's bay, is by boat or on foot. The best rooms are at the top, and they have roof terraces.A great place to stay to get away from it all.
✉ Loutró, Hóra Sfakión, Haniá ☎ 28250 91433; fax 28250 91091 ⛴ Regular boat from Agía Roméli and Hóra Sfakión

Réthymno

RÉTHYMNO TOWN

FORTÉZZA (€€)
Centrally located, and close to the old fort, this stylish hotel in the centre of town has its own swimming pool and garden courtyard. All rooms have air conditioning and balconies.

✉ Odós Melissinoú 16
☎ 28310 23828; fax: 28310 54073

GRECOTEL RÉTHYMNA BEACH HOTEL AND BUNGALOWS (€€€)
On the beach 7km northeast of Réthymno, this huge luxury complex is highly popular with families. Altogether there are around 600 rooms, some in the main hotel buildings, others in bungalows and villas. The range of amenities includes restaurants, pools, watersports and fitness club and there is plenty on offer for children, including supervised camping on the beach.

✉ Adele Beach, Réthymno
☎ 28310 71002; fax: 28310 71668

HOTEL LÉON (€)
This 500-year-old house, has 11 simple rooms, all with shower, and its own café/bar. It lies in the heart of the old town and preserves its Venetian character.

✉ Odós Vafé 4 ☎ 28310 26197

IDÉON (€€)
Good value hotel, well placed for the centre of the city and the Venetian harbour. It was built in

the 1970s and offers 95 modern rooms with air-conditioning, a swimming pool and a restaurant. Try to get a room with a sea view.

✉ Plateía Plastíra 10
☎ 28310 28667; fax: 28310 28670

MÍNOS MARE (€€€)
Large, modern hotel standing on the sand and shingle beach of Plataniás, 5km from Réthymno. Ideal for all ages, with pools, gym, sauna, evening entertainment and children's facilities. Guests can also use the facilities of the sister hotel, the Mínos, 3km away.

✉ Platanias, Réthymno
☎ 28310 50388; fax 28310 53310

AGÍA GALÍNI

HOTEL LITÓ (€)
This is a small family hotel in a pretty residential street and conveniently placed close to the centre and harbour. There are ten simple, clean rooms, all with private bathrooms.

✉ Agía Galíni, Réthymno
☎ 28320 91231

PLAKIÁS

NÉOS ALIÁNTHOS (€€)
Family-run, informal hotel across the road from the beach of Plakiás. The hotel has 94 bedrooms on two floors and an outdoor freshwater pool. Plakiás' shops, bars and tavernas are a few minutes' walk away.

✉ Plakiás, Réthymno
☎ 28320 31280; fax: 28320 31282

HOTEL STARS

Greek hotels are currently classified into six grades, starting with deluxe (L) and going down from Category A through to the very basic Category E. A list of hotels on Crete is available from overseas offices of the Greek National Tourist Organisation (known as the EOT or GNTO).

RURAL HIDEAWAY

High season in Miliá (€€) is the winter when log fires burn and guests are plied with free *rakí* and hot chestnuts. This is alternative Crete, idyllic for nature lovers and a far cry from the tourist fleshpots of the coast. The village has 12 rustic stone dwellings, lit by oil lamps (no electricity) and supplied with organic food from the land – rabbits, chickens, lambs, honey and wine.

✉ Miliá, near Vlátos Kissámou
☎ 28220 51569

Markets

WHEN AND WHERE

Shop opening hours vary widely according to the place and season. Officially shops open on Monday, Wednesday and Saturday from 8 or 9am–1.30 or 2pm, and on Tuesday, Thursday and Friday the same hours, but reopening from 5 or 5.30pm–8 or 8.30pm. Shops for tourists, however, tend to be open all day seven days a week, often until 10pm or 11pm. Some tourist shops close completely during the winter or open for shorter hours. The largest concentration of shops are in Iráklio, Réthymno, Haniá and Ágios Nikólaos.

IRÁKLIO OPEN MARKET

A stroll along Odós 1866 any morning of the week will give you an idea of the wealth of produce from Crete's fertile valleys and hothouses. Bustling, colourful and crowded, the market retains some of the flavour of the former oriental bazaar under the Turks and Venetians. Stalls are piled high with fresh fruit and vegetables: peppers, aubergines, beans, zucchini, peaches, cherries and melons – to name just a few. Butchers shops are hung with whole carcasses and strings of sausages, leather stalls with bags and belts, small shops with brightly woven rugs and embroidered linen. Grocery shops and stalls are crammed with baskets of spices, jars of wild herb honey, Cretan mountain tea, olives and nuts, goat and sheep's cheeses. As well as culinary delights there are souvenirs such as sponges and Cretan knives, and everyday goods such as wooden spoons, copper coffee pots, knives or hand-made leather boots. Having soaked up the atmosphere and struck your bargains, why not relax and sit at the café of the Turkish pumphouse in Plateía Kornarou at the end of the street or one of the small tavernas in the side street to the east where many of the marketholders take their meals.

✉ Odós 1866, Iráklio 🕒 Mon, Wed, Sat 8–2, Tue, Thu, Fri 8–2, 5–8.30

HANIÁ MARKET

The splendid market hall, which provides a cool retreat from the street in summer, was built in 1913. Cruciform in shape, it was designed on the lines of the marketplace in Marseilles. The spectacle of herbs and honeys, oils and spices, dried fruits, cheese, fish, meat, fruit and vegetables is every bit as alluring and lively as the market in Iráklio. This is the perfect place to buy your picnic or beach snack: pastries filled with feta cheese or wild greens, sweet tomatoes, olives, peaches, figs and bottles of Cretan wine. Be sure to try the cheeses before you buy. Stallholders will encourage you to taste each variety and tell you where they are made. Look out for *kouloúra* – the dried, elaborately decorated Cretan wedding bread, which can be taken home as souvenirs. Insect repellent, applied every three months, preserves the bread.

✉ Plateía Sophokles Venizélos 🕒 Mon, Wed, Thu, Sat 8–2, Tue, Fri 8.30–1.30, 5–8 (summer 6–9)

OTHER MARKETS

Iráklio also has a Saturday morning market by the port. This is less atmospheric than the town's street market, but sells a wide variety of goods including food and clothes. Other main towns such as Réthymno, Ágios Nikólaos and Sitía have markets during the week, but on a small scale beside those of Iráklio and Haniá.

Arts, Crafts & Souvenirs

JEWELLERY
The main towns offer a wide choice of gold and silver jewellery, some of it very stylish. There are also some beautiful reproductions of Minoan jewellery wrought in gold and other metals. In Iráklio, Odós Daedálou is the best source for good-quality jewellery.

WORRY BEADS
Greeks fiddle with worry beads or *kombolói* as a way of relaxing. These are popular bought as souvenirs and are available from tourist shops, markets or jewellers.

WINES AND SPIRITS
You never have to go far to find a shop selling Greek wines and spirits. Crete produces its own wine (red and white) *retsina* (resinated wine) and *rakí* (spirit). You can also buy cheap Greek brandy and *ouzo*, an aniseed-flavoured spirit similar to Pernod.

IRÁKLIO PROVINCE

IRÁKLIO TOWN

AERÁKIS
One of the oldest record stores in Crete and now dwarfed by both a Virgin Megastore and Metropolis Records, Aerákis specialises in Cretan music with many records released on his own label, some dating back as far as 1920.
✉ Odós Daedálou
☎ 2810 225758

ELÉNI KASTRINOYÁNNI
Opposite the Archaeological Museum, Helen Kastrinoyanni's shop specialises in Cretan handwoven embroideries, rugs, woven linen, jewellery and reproductions of clay figurines that you may well recognise if you have already visited the museum.
✉ Plateía Eleftherías 1
☎ 2810 226186

FANOURÁKIS
Pávlos Fanourákis, a renowned jeweller from Crete, also has shops in Athens where his unique designs have proven very popular.
✉ Platéia Nik. Foká
☎ 2810 282708

MOUSTÁKIS
High quality leather shoes and boots for men and women. Although the stock is made in Greece, it is not cheap.
✉ Odós Daedálou 3
☎ 2810 240109

NAFTÍLOS
An interesting bookshop, albeit most of the stock is in Greek, however there is a good selection of prints and engravings reflecting Iráklio's past.
✉ Odós Koraí 4 ☎ No phone

LASSÍTHI PROVINCE

ÁGIÓS NIKÓLAOS

BYZÁNTIO
Most of the icons here are hand-painted and the artist who works here will explain the techniques,

WHAT TO BUY
The best buys are traditional crafts – brightly coloured handwoven textiles, jewellery, ceramics, sculpture and leatherware. Although some of the 'crafts' sold in tourist areas are mass-produced and cheaply made, you still occasionally come across women working at looms, potters at the wheel or leather craftsmen making traditional knee-length boots.

77

LEATHER

Shops all over Crete sell leather goods, most of them made in Greece. Daidálos Street in Iráklio has very stylish shoes and leather jackets, but for cheaper leatherwork (bags, boots, belts, wallets) try the market in Iráklio, and Odós Skrídlof in Haniá which is entirely devoted to leather stalls. Villagers come here to buy handmade knee-length boots – fine quality but no bargain.

POTTERY

The villages of Margarítes (east of Réthymno) and Thrápsano (15km southeast of Kastélli, Iráklio) are long-established pottery-making centres, where you can visit the workshops and watch potters using ancient techniques. Some of them still make *pithária*, the giant storage pots made on Crete since Minoan times. Not the ideal purchase to take back on the plane, but there are plenty of smaller souvenirs, and prices are lower than those of the shops.

such as the cracking of the gold leaf to get the antique look. All of them are copies from old churches and monasteries throughout Greece. The icons come signed and with a certificate.
✉ Odós 28 Oktovríou 14
☎ 28410 26530

CERAMICÁ 1

Nic Gabriel keeps the spirit of traditional Greek forms alive with his hand-made copies of ceramics from museums all over Greece. Each piece comes with a certificate of provenance and information about the history of the original. Shipping can be arranged.
✉ Odós Paleológou 28
☎ 28410 24075

MARÍA PATSÁKI

In a resort where so many shops sell souvenirs, this one stands out for its beautiful hand-woven textiles. Maria Patsaki has been here for 20 years, selling hand-woven bedcovers, rugs, carpets and beautiful fabrics that can be bought by the metre or made up to order (bedsets take two or three days and purchases can be sent abroad).
✉ Odós K. Sfakianákis, 2
☎ 28410 22001

ZOÉ

A good place to come for fun designer T-shirts for all ages decorated with motifs from Greek mythology. The shop, which is one of a chain, is English-run.
✉ Odós Paleólogou 1 (by the lake) ☎ 28410 23352

ELOÚNDA

PETRÁKIS ICON WORKSHOP

Artists Yiorgia and Ioannis Petrákis create beautifully painted icons using traditional materials and methods on Eloúnda's main street. Prices are very reasonable. They also sell a tasteful range of sculptures, jewellery and ceramics.
✉ Odós A. Papandréou 22, Eloúnda ☎ 28410 41669

HANIÁ PROVINCE

HANIÁ TOWN

PARÁ ORO

A workshop specialising in hand-made objects of art. Stamatis works wonders with materials such as metal and glass, crafting unique creations.
✉ Odós Theotokopoúlou 16
☎ 28210 88990

CARMÉLA

This is more like a gallery than a shop. Carmela and her husband create beautiful ceramics and paintings, and there are original works of art from all over Greece made using traditional techniques.
✉ Odós Angélou 7 ☎ 28210 90487

DIÓNYSOS CELLAR

Located in an old Venetian town house, this shop has been owned and run by the Kassimátis family for around 80 years. They specialise in high quality local products including olive oil, herbs, honey and a good range of

drinks, including local wine, *ouzo*, *metaxa* and *rakí*. They also stock attractive local ceramics.
✉ Odós Theotokopoúlou 63 ☎ 28210 27722

LEATHER LANE
The street is almost entirely devoted to leather stalls. Choose from bags, belts, wallets, shoes, slippers and leather souvenirs. Much of it is made on the premises and the prices are reasonable.
✉ Odós Skrídlof

LOCAL ARTISTIC HANDICRAFTS' ASSOCIATION
Craft items by 40 local artists displayed in a 200-year old building on Haniá's harbour. The exhibits are not for sale, but staff will put you in touch with the workshops where they are made. Range includes ceramics, jewellery, embroidery, glass, knives, semi-precious stones and bronze characters from Greek mythology.
✉ Odós Afedoúlief 14, Old Harbour ☎ 28210 41885

RÓKA CARPETS
Wonderful selection of kilims, rugs and carpets – all hand-made by loom. If the shop is closed in winter knock on the door – except Sundays, which is the day for dying the wool.
✉ Odós Zambelíou 61 ☎ 28210 74736

TOP HANÁS
Richly coloured, hand-woven Cretan bedspreads, kilims and tapestries,

some of them over 100 years old, hung within an old Venetian building. Many of these were made for dowries.
✉ Odós Angélou 3–5 (near the Naval Museum) ☎ 28210 98571

RÉTHYMNO TOWN

21
For a wide selection of jewellery, including necklaces, brooches and bracelets made on the premises by the owner Aristídes, it is worth a visit to his workshop in a quaint alleyway in the Old Town area of Réthymno.
✉ Odós Souliou 21, Réthymno ☎ No phone

BROTHERS KIMIONÍS
A family business operating since 1908, the Brothers Kimionis was the first shop to sell *rakí* in Crete. Today you'll find this a gourmet's delight packed with all kinds of spices, olive oils, honey, herbs and Cretan dictamus tea. Browsers may be lucky enough to be given a glass of *rakí* or a taste of local honey, but there is no obligation to buy.
✉ Odós Paleológou 29–31, Réthymno ☎ 28310 55667

KÁLYMNOS
Sponges of all shapes and sizes fill this delightful corner shop in the heart of the shopping district. Most of the stock comes from the Greek seas and lasts longer than cheaper varieties from other countries.
✉ Odós Aravatzóglou 26, Réthymno ☎ 28310 50802

HERBS AND SPICES
Neatly packaged baskets of Cretan herbs and spices, sold in markets and food shops, make ideal gifts. Or take back some of the delicious aromatic Cretan honey, often sold in jars with nuts. Brothers Kimionís (➤ this page) in Odós Paleólogou, Réthymno, is an excellent place to shop for these. A family business since 1908, it is a gourmet's delight.

ICONS
For a souvenir with a difference buy a Greek icon. These can be found all over the island and are normally reproductions of originals from churches and monasteries throughout Greece. The originals are hard to come by – and it's illegal to take them home.

Bars, Discos, Clubs & Music

BRIGHT LIGHTS

Limín Hersónisou and Mália are the party capitals of Crete, with numerous neon-signed late-night bars and discos. Haniá's nightlife is concentrated around the harbour, with cocktail bars and live Greek or international music in cafés and tavernas; Réthymno has its fare share of discos and music bars; and Ágios Nikólaos' harbour is the scene of lively, late-night bars and discos. However it should be noted that many bars and discos change hands frequently and this usually involves a change of name – so don't be surprised if the premises are not called what you expected. Opening times are often seasonal and varied – check first.

IRÁKLIO PROVINCE

ARÓLITHOS

Open-air Cretan evenings with live music and dancing in full traditional costume. This takes place in a cleverly constructed 'traditional' Cretan village in the hills near Týlisos, where you can watch the local artisans in their workshops and buy their handmade goods.
✉ PO Box 2032 N Stadium 71002 (11km southwest of Iráklio on the Old National Road) ☎ 2810 821050; fax: 2810 821051

CAMELOT

One of many discos in the late-night resort of Limín Hersonísou. You won't find many Cretans here but young tourists love it. Good music and dancing.
✉ Odós Mínoos 9, Limín Hersónisou ☎ 28970 22734

KAROUZÁNOS EVENING

Excursions are organised to the traditional mountain village of Karouzános, near Kastélli. The evenings start with a glass of *rakí*, followed by a walk around the village, a drink in a *kafeníon* (traditional café) and a typical Cretan dinner in a local taverna, with free-flowing wine. The meal is accompanied by Cretan and Greek dancing.
Information from: ✉ Káto Karouzaná, Pediádos, Iráklio ☎ 28910 32404; fax: 28910 32329 or ✉ International Travel Service S. A. Odós Daedálou 36, Iráklio ☎ 2810 228413; fax: 2810 223851

KAZANTZÁKIS THEATRE

This is an open-air venue for concerts, theatre and dance during Iráklio's summer festival. Some free performances. The festival director is Yiógos Antonákis (☎ 2810 299211; fax: 2810 229207).
✉ Jesus Bastion, near the Oasis Gardens, Iráklio ☎ 2810 242977; fax: 2810 227180

LION'S BAR

Called the Last Bar Before Africa (it would be if it weren't for the island of Gávdos), Lion's Bar has wonderful views of the sunset (and the sunrise). Twenty-one cocktails, music of all types and impromptu dancing. Meals are available here until late.
✉ Mátala Beach, Mátala ☎ 28920 45108

PLATÉIA KORAÍ

Platéia Koraí is the liveliest place in the town for an evening drink and is popular with young people. There are several casual bars with tables on the square, serving cocktails and other drinks. You will find a mix of international and modern Greek music.
✉ Platéia Koraí, Iráklio

PRIVILEGE

This sizeable and popular club has been packing them in since 1998. It is open every night throughout the summer with a variety of guest D.J.'s.
✉ Odós Doukós Bofór 7, Iráklio ☎ 2810 244850

LASSÍTHI PROVINCE

SALÓME
Kóstas has been running this individual bar now for 20 years. In the months of July and August there is live Greek and international music every night, often with Kóstas himself, an accomplished guitarist.
✉ Odós M. Sfakianáki 7, Ágios Nikólaos ☎ 28410 26913

YÁNNI'S ROCK MUSIC BAR
Great music at this small, down-to-earth club at the end of the harbour, from classic 1970s and 80s rock to hard rock and blues.
✉ Ákti Iosíf Koúndourou, Ágios Nikólaos

HANIÁ PROVINCE

KONÁKI
A taverna located in the Old Town with live Greek music.
✉ Odós Kondiláki 40, Haniá ☎ 28210 97130

KRÍTI
Simple café near the Arsenal where you can listen to local music, and, if the mood takes you no one will stop you throwing caution to the wind and partaking of an impromptu dance.
✉ Odós Kallergón 22, Haniá ☎ None

MUSIC BAR POINT
On the first floor overlooking the Old Harbour, Aléxis has been running this lively bar for more years than he cares to remember. One of Haniá's few classic bars it survives due to a good choice in music and an excellent sound system.
✉ Sourméli 2, Old Harbour, Haniá ☎ 28210 57556

RÉTHYMNO PROVINCE

PUNCH BOWL IRISH BAR
Popular pub in a pretty street of the old town, serving Guinness, Amstel, Irish coffee and a long list of cocktails. Get there early for happy Hour (drinks at half price) from 8pm–10pm.
✉ Odós Aravatzóglou 42, Réthymno ☎ 28310 55572

RÉTHYMNO FESTIVAL
Every summer, concerts, theatrical performances, ballet, recitals, traditional dance and song are performed as part of the Renaissance Festival at the Erofíli Theatre in the the Venetian fortress. Other performances at the Réthymno Odéon (Music School) at the Neratzé Mosque. The telephone numbers given below are applicable from one hour prior to performance.
✉ Erofíli Theatre: Odós Katehaki, Réthymno ☎ 28310 28101
✉ Réthymno Odéon: Old Town, Réthymno ☎ 28310 22724

ROCK CAFÉ CLUB
It's always good to see that locals and foreigners mix happily at this popular dance club in the heart of town.
✉ Odós Petiháki 8, Réthymno ☎ 28310 31047

CRETAN MUSIC
Cretans love to get up and dance and usually ensure that tourists all join in. The best-known instruments of Cretan folk music are the *lýra*, a pear-shaped instrument played with a bow, accompanied by the *laoúto*, which is like a very big mandolin and has a deep bass sound. Normally the fancier the venue, the less authentic the performance.

SUMMER FESTIVAL
Every summer the city council of Haniá organises a wide variety of events including theatre, dance, music and exhibitions in a number of venues. The principal space is the Theátro Anatolikís Táfrou (The Eastern Moat Theatre) by the old town wall. Further information from Níkos Perákis (☎ 28210 87098/87077; fax 28210 74332).

Participatory Sports

MELTÉMÍ

Beware of the strong dry northerly wind known as the *Meltémi*, likely to hit Crete any time between June and September. The wind lingers for several days causing a drop in temperature, choppy seas and seaweed-strewn beaches.

FENNY'S GUIDED WALKING TOUR OF HANIÁ OLD TOWN

Tony Fennymore undertakes 2-hour walking tours from April until the end of June and September to the end of October. He is a wealth of information about Haniá's history and sites. Tours cost €12 per person (☎/fax 28210 87139; Mob: 697 253 7055; e-mail : fennyscrete@hotmail.com) His reader-friendly, companion book for the tour – *Fenny's Haniá* (€7.50) – is available from his website (www.fennyscrete.ws) and in many bookshops in the town.

CYCLING

Hiring a bike is a pleasant way of exploring the island, but the hills and mountains make for strenuous pedalling. Cycle excursion companies can take away the strain by transporting the bikes up the mountains, allowing you to enjoy the scenic ride down. The cycling distances of the different excursions range from about 25 to 50km. The routes are mainly on surfaced roads and the cost includes guide, mountain bike, crash helmets, picnic and drinks.
Trekking Plan Outdoor Activities (for mountain bike hire and bike excursions) ✉ Agía Marina, Kidonia, Haniá ☎ 28210 60861; fax: 28210 60785

DIVING

The warmth and crystal clear waters of the Cretan seas make excellent conditions for diving. Among the marine flora and fauna you are likely to see are sea anemones, sponges, small crabs, starfish, rock fish, octopus and moray eels. The waters are also excellent for snorkelling, and equipment can be hired or bought locally.

SCUBAKRETA DIVE CENTER

This well-equipped club organises a full range of regular PADI (Professional Association of Diving Instructors) courses. The taster session for the total beginner is a one-day course consisting of theory-pool dive and a sea dive to a maximum of 5–6m. The 4–5 day PADI full certificate course includes theory, confined water training and four sea dives. Divers with PADI or other internationally recognised certificates can participate in night diving, deep diving, cave diving or photo dives. The standards of safety are high, whether you are doing your first dive off the seashore or plunging 40m to the depths of the Mediterranean. The attractions include sunken wrecks and a variety of marine life.
✉ Nana Beach Hotel, Limín Hersónisou ☎ 28970 24915; fax: 28970 24916

GOLF

Currently the only opportunity for golfers is the 9-hole course at the Porto Eloúnda Resort, where tuition is available. There are plans in the pipeline to build several new golf courses on the island.
✉ Porto Eloúnda Resort, Eloúnda, Lassíthi ☎ 28410 68200; fax: 28410 41889

HORSE RIDING

Horse riding and riding lessons are available at clubs in or near the four main centres of Iráklio, Ágios Nikólaos, Réthymno and Haniá.

CLUB KARTERÓS

Opportunities for exploring the countryside on horseback. Also riding lessons and horse and wagon tours.
✉ Amnisós-Karterós beach, Iráklio ☎ 2810 380244

DERÈS HORSE-RIDING CENTRE

In a remote location, this riding centre offers accompanied tours in the mountains. Café and restaurant.

✉ Derès, Haniá ☎ 28240 31339 fax: 28240 31900

WALKING AND CLIMBING

With its scenic gorges, mountains and valleys Crete provides plenty of opportunities for walking and climbing. The most famous walk is the 16km Samariá Gorge (➤ 17, 33). Less crowded and half the length are the Ímbros Gorge (➤ 32) and the Agía Irini Gorge. Only serious climbers should tackle the Lefká Óri (White Mountains) or Crete's highest peak, Timíos Stavrós (2,456m).

GREEK CLIMBING CLUB (EOS)

The club operates refuges in the White Mountains (☎ 28210 54560) and at Psiloreítis. It also has information on skiing in the Cretan mountains.

✉ Odós Dikaiosínis 53, Iráklio ☎ 2810 227609
✉ Odós Tzanakákis 90, Haniá ☎ 28210 74560
✉ Odós Dimokratías 12, Réthymno ☎ 28310 57766

THE HAPPY WALKER

Six different walks, organised in small groups led by an experienced guide. The walks last about four hours and end with lunch at a taverna. Transport is provided to the starting point.

✉ Odós Tobázi, 56, Réthymno (in the old town, near the Metropolis church) ☎ 28310 52920

NATURE MANIACS

Nature Maniacs organise and carry out nature, adventure and cultural trips in western Crete providing sea-kayaking, caving, climbing, trekking and sailing. Their goal is to provide high-quality outdoor recreational activities that empower individuals to grow physically, mentally and spiritually, enhancing their quality of life and fostering a passion for the outdoors.

✉ 1st Floor, above the chemist and the sub Post Office on the High Street, Plataniás Village, Haniá ☎ 28210 60001

WATERSPORTS AND SWIMMING

The sandy beaches and warm, clear waters are excellent for swimming. The main season for watersports is from late May to late October. The larger resort beaches, such as Mália, Ágios Nikólaos and the strip west of Haniá, offer a choice of watersports such as windsurfing (with instruction and board-hire), pedaloes, banana boats and jet skis.

SOFITÉL CAPSÍS PALACE AND CAPSÍS BEACH RESORT HOTEL

✉ Ágia Pelagía
☎ 2810 811212; fax: 2810 811076

ELOÚNDA BEACH HOTEL

✉ 72100 Ágios Nikólaos
☎ 28410 41412; fax: 28410 41373

DIVING

To protect antiquities, diving independently of a club in Greek waters is forbidden. Half a dozen specific areas in Crete are exempt from the ban including Eloúnda (information from Eloúnda Beach Hotel, ☎ 28410 41412) and Réthymno (information from Paradise Dive Centre, El Venizélou, 73 ☎ 28310 26317). Divers are strictly forbidden to remove any antiquities from the sea bed, or even to take photographs of them.

SPIRIT OF CRETE

Tim Powell can act as your personal assistant whilst you are on the island. If you are in need of a driver, interpreter or general factotum then Tim is your man. With 20 years experience of the island, he is bi-lingual (Greek/English) and can show you a multitude of fascinating places off the tourist trail as well as the past and present everyday life of the Cretans. Contact him at: timbasse@yahoo.co.uk

CRETE
practical matters

WHAT YOU NEED

		UK	Germany	USA	Netherlands	Spain
● Required ○ Suggested ▲ Not required	Some countries require a passport to remain valid for a minimum period (usually at least six months) beyond the date of entry — contact their consulate or embassy or your travel agent for details.					
Passport/National Identity Card		●	●	●	●	●
Visa (regulations can change – check before you travel)		▲	▲	▲	▲	▲
Onward or Return Ticket		▲	▲	▲	▲	▲
Health Inoculations (tetanus and polio)		○	○	○	○	○
Health Documentation (reciprocal agreement: ➤ 90, Health)		●	●	▲	●	●
Travel Insurance		●	●	●	●	●
Driving Licence (National or International; EU nationals need national licence only)		●	●	●	●	●
Car Insurance Certificate (if own car)		●	●	●	●	●
Car Registration Document (if own car)		●	●	●	●	●

WHEN TO GO

Crete

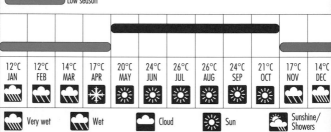

High season

Low season

12°C JAN	12°C FEB	14°C MAR	17°C APR	20°C MAY	24°C JUN	26°C JUL	26°C AUG	24°C SEP	21°C OCT	17°C NOV	14°C DEC

Very wet   Wet   Cloud   Sun   Sunshine/Showers

TIME DIFFERENCES

GMT 12 noon	Crete 2pm	Germany 1pm	USA (NY) 7am	Netherlands 1pm	Spain 1pm

TOURIST OFFICES

In the UK
Greek National Tourist
Organisation (GNTO)
4 Conduit Street
London, W1S 2DJ
☎ 020 7734 5997
Fax: 020 7287 1369
www.gnto.gr

In the USA
GNTO
Olympic Tower
645 Fifth Avenue
New York, NY10022
☎ 212/421 5777
Fax: 212/826 6940
www.greektourism.com

In Canada
GNTO/EOT
1170 Place du Frère André
Suite 300
Montréal, Quebec
H3B 3C6
☎ 514/871 1535
Fax: 514/871 1498

ARRIVING

The majority of direct flights to Crete are charters from major European cities, available only from April to October. Tour operators fly mainly to Iráklio, though some also use Haniá airport for resorts in western Crete. There are scheduled flights to Athens from Europe and the USA, with connections to Crete.

Iráklio Airport
Kilometres to city centre

5 kilometres

Journey times

🚇	N/A
🚌	15 minutes
🚗	10 minutes

Haniá Airport
Kilometres to city centre

12 kilometres

Journey times

🚇	N/A
🚌	20 minutes
🚗	15 minutes

MONEY

On January 1, 2002, Greece adopted the euro and the Greek drachma was withdrawn. Euro notes come in denominations of 500, 200, 100, 50, 20, 10 and 5; coins in denominations of 2 and 1 euros, 50, 20, 10, 5, 2 and one cents. Foreign currencies and travellers' cheques can be exchanged at banks, bureaux de change and travel agents. Visa, MasterCard and Eurocard are widely accepted in the main resorts and can be used to take out cash from ATM machines at most banks.

TIME

 Crete is two hours ahead of Greenwich Mean Time (GMT + 2). The clocks go forward one hour on the last Sunday in March and back one hour on the last Sunday in October.

CUSTOMS

 YES

From another EU country for personal use (guidelines)
800 cigarettes
200 cigars
1 kilogram of tobacco
10 litres of spirits (over 22%)
20 litres of aperitifs
90 litres of wine, of which 60 litres can be sparkling wine
110 litres of beer

From a non-EU country for your personal use, the allowances are:
200 cigarettes OR
50 cigars OR
250 grams of tobacco
1 litre of spirits (over 22 %)
2 litres of intermediary products (eg sherry) and sparkling wine
2 litres of still wine
50 grams of perfume
0.25 litres of eau de toilette
The value limit for goods is €175

Travellers under 17 years of age are not entitled to the tobacco and alcohol allowances.

 NO

Drugs, firearms, ammunition, offensive weapons, obscene material, unlicensed animals.

CONSULATES

UK
☎ 2810 224012
(Iráklio)

Germany
☎ 2810 226288
(Iráklio) 28210 68875
(Haniá)

USA
☎ (Athens Embassy)
210 721 2951

Netherlands
☎ 2810 346202
(Iráklio)

TOURIST OFFICES

● **Iráklio**
Odós Papa Alexándrou E 16, Iráklio
☎ 2810 246106; fax: 2810
246105
Information Office
Odós Ksanthoudídou 1
☎ 2810 246299; fax: 2810
246105

Iráklio Airport
Iráklio
☎ 2810 397305

● **Ágios Nikólaos**
Odós Akti Koúndourou, 20 (between the lake and the harbour), Ágios Nikólaos, Lassíthi
☎ 28410 22357; fax:28410 82534

● **Haniá**
Odós Kriári 40, Mégaro Pántheon, Haniá
☎ 28210 92943; fax: 28210
92624

● **Réthymno**
Odós Elefthérios Venizélos (on the seafront east of the harbour), Réthymno
☎ 28310 29148; fax: 28310
56350

EMAIL & INTERNET

All the major towns and most of the tourist areas in Crete have Internet cafés in abundance, often open into the early hours, including:

Perípou Polihóros
Odós 28th Octovríou 25, Ágios Nikólaos
☎ 28410 24876

W. W. W.,
Odós Balantínou 4, Haniá
☎ 28210 93478

ELECTRICITY

The power supply in Greece is 220 volts AC, 50 Hz.

Sockets accept two-round-pin continental-style plugs. Visitors from the UK require a plug adaptor and US visitors will need a transformer for appliances operating on 100–120 volts.

NATIONAL HOLIDAYS

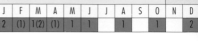

J	F	M	A	M	J	J	A	S	O	N	D
2	(1)	1(2)	(1)	1	1		1		1		2

1 Jan	New Year's Day
6 Jan	Epiphany
End Feb/early Mar	Clean Monday
25 March	Independence Day
Mar/Apr	Good Friday and Easter
May 1	Labour Day
May/Jun	Ascension Day
Aug 15	Feast of the Assumption
Oct 28	Óchi Day
25 Dec	Christmas Day
26 Dec	St Stephen's Day

Restaurants and some tourists shops may stay open on these days, but museums will be closed.

OPENING HOURS

○ Shops	● Post Offices
● Offices	● Museums
● Banks	● Pharmacies

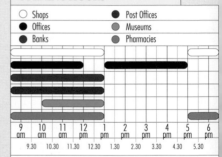

9 am	10 am	11 am	12 pm	1 pm	2 pm	3 pm	4 pm	5 pm	6 pm
9.30	10.30	11.30	12.30	1.30	2.30	3.30	4.30	5.30	

In addition to the times shown above, many shops in tourist areas stay open daily from 8am to late evening throughout the season but close or have shorter hours in winter (➤ 76).
Many restaurants stay open all day during the holiday season (➤ 64).
Post offices in Iráklio and Haniá are open 7.30–7.30. Banks close on Saturdays, Sundays and public holidays.
The opening hours of museums and archaeological sites vary enormously but the majority are closed on Mondays (➤ 12).

TIPS/GRATUITIES

Yes ✓	No ✗		
Hotels (if service not inc.)		✓	10%
Restaurants (service included)		✓	change
Cafés/bars (if service not included)		✓	10%
Taxis		✓	change
Tour guides		✓	discretionary
Porters		✓	€1–€2
Chambermaids		✓	discretionary
Hairdressers		✓	10%
Toilets		✓	discretionary

PUBLIC TRANSPORT

 Island Buses Crete has an extensive network of buses, providing a cheap and reasonably reliable service throughout the island. There is an excellent service along the main highway linking Ágios Nikólaos, Iráklio, Réthymno and Haniá, with buses at least every hour. From these towns there are services to smaller towns and most villages. Iráklio has three bus stations, operating services to different regions. Only buses within Iráklio are numbered – others show the destination (not always the right one) on the front of the bus. Local bus timetables are available from bus stations, local tourist offices and sometimes at bus stops. You need to flag down the bus as it approaches.

 Ferries connect Iráklio, Haniá and Ágios Nikólaos with the mainland at Piraeus (Port of Athens) and with other islands such as Rhodes and Santorini. Boat excursions operate from May to October. Popular trips include cruises to the offshore islands of Spinalónga, Gaïdouronísi (Chrisí) and Diá. Ferries link the south coast resorts of Palaeóchora, Soúgia, Agía Rouméli, Loutró and Hora Sfakíon. From Soúgia, Palaeóchora and Hora Sfakíon ferries operate to the island of Gávdos south of Crete.
Boat trips are avilable from Kastélli Kissámou to Gramvoúsa, and from several resorts to unspoilt and otherwise inaccessible beaches.

 Urban Transport Iráklio is the only major conurbation on Crete but because of the one-way system and the central location of the sites and shops, most tourists tend to walk. The city has three bus stations, operating services to different regions of Crete. Buses for Knossós leave from a stop adjacent to the east-bound bus station.

CAR RENTAL

 Crete has numerous car rental firms, including all the internationally known names. Hire rates are generally reasonable by European standards, particularly off-season. Check they include tax, collision damage waivers and unlimited mileage.

TAXIS

 Taxis on Crete are plentiful and can be hailed in the street or picked up at taxi ranks. Check the meter is switched on or, if there is no meter, agree a price in advance. There are some fixed price journeys within towns and from the airports

CONCESSIONS

Students/Youths – Holders of an International Student Identity Card (ISIC) are entitled to substantial reductions on entrance fees to museums and archaeological sites. Very cheap accommodation is available in youth hostels at Iráklio, Ágios Nikólaos, Réthymno, Haniá, Sitía and other towns, but early reservations for the summer months are essential.

Senior Citizens – Most museums and archaeological sites have reduced rates for elderly visitors although proof is often asked for. There are few other concessions but senior citizens can take advantage of the off-season rates in spring and October – the ideal times to visit the island.

DRIVING

 Speed limit on national highways:
100kph

 Speed limit on outside built-up areas:
80kph

 Speed limit in built-up areas:
50kph

 Must be worn in front seats and in the rear where fitted. Children under 10 years are not allowed in the front seat.

 Random breath-testing. Never drive under the influence of alcohol.

 Petrol is readily available in the towns, but it's wise to fill up if you are touring. Super (95 octane), unleaded, super unleaded and diesel are available. Service stations are open Mon–Fri, 7am–7pm, Sat 7am–3pm. Some stay open until midnight and open Sun 7am–7pm.

 Members of motoring organisations are entitled to free breakdown service from the Greek motoring organisation, ELPA ☎ 10400 in emergencies. Car hire companies should also be notified as most will have their own procedures.

PHOTOGRAPHY

 Where it is forbidden: in some museums, near military bases and in churches and monasteries where icons require flash.
Film and Digital: Due to the advent of digital cameras, films are becoming somewhat harder to find. Camera shops of course still stock the most popular speeds but if you want to use a fast film or slide film it is better to stock up in advance. Most of these shops now offer a service for burning memory cards on to CD.

PERSONAL SAFETY

The crime rate in Crete is very low. Visitors can stroll through the streets without any threat, though unescorted women should not be surprised if they attract the Mediterranean roving eye. Whilst petty crime is minimal, it's wise to take simple precautions:
● Safeguard against attracting the attention of pickpockets.
● Leave valuables and important documents in the hotel or apartment safe.
● Lock car doors and never leave valuables visible inside.

Police assistance:
☎ **100**
from any call box

TELEPHONES

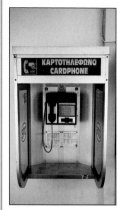

Public telephones take a phone card, available locally in units of 100, 200, 500 and 1,000. Some kiosks, shops and cafés have telephones with meters that can be used for international calls. OTE (Greek Telecom) have telephone exchanges in the larger resorts where you can make calls from booths and pay in cash afterwards.

International Dialling Codes

From Crete to:	
UK:	00 44
Germany:	00 49
USA:	00 1

POST

Post Offices

Post offices in the towns and larger villages are identified by yellow signs. In summer mobile offices operate in tourist areas. Post offices usually open 7.30–2.30 Mon–Fri, but in Iráklio and Haniá they're open until 7.30. Some mobile post offices also open at weekends. Stamps can be bought at shops or kiosks selling postcards.

HEALTH

Medical Treatment

Visitors from the European Union (EU) are entitled to reciprocal state medical care in Greece and should take with them the EHIC card (European Health Insurance Card) available from post offices. However, this covers treatment in only the most basic of hospitals and private medical insurance is advisable.

Dental Services

Dental treatment must be paid for by all visitors. Hotels can normally provide names of local English-speaking dentists; alternatively ask your Consulate. Private medical insurance is strongly advised to cover the cost of dental treatment.

Sun Advice

Crete enjoys sunshine for most of the year, and from April/May until September it is almost constant. During July and August, when the sun is at its hottest, a hat, strong-protection sunscreen and plenty of non-alcoholic fluids are recommended.

Drugs

Pharmacies have a large green or red cross outside the shop and sell most internationally known drugs and medicines over the counter or by prescription. Most pharmacies have someone who can speak English. Opening hours are the same as those of shops, with a rota system at weekends.

Safe Water

Tap water is generally safe although in remoter areas or on the south coast it is best to ask before drinking it. However, due to the high level of minerals, it may not suit all visitors but bottled water is available everywhere at reasonable prices.

LANGUAGE

The official language of Crete is Greek. Many of the locals speak English, but a few words of Greek can be useful in rural areas where locals may know no English. It is also useful to know the Greek alphabet – particularly for reading street names and road signs. A few useful words and phrases are listed below, with phonetic transliterations and accents to show emphasis. More words and phrases can be found in the AA Essential Greek Phrase Book. Because the method of translating Greek place names has changed recently, some spellings may differ from older ones you find on the island.

hotel	*xenodhohío*	toilet	*twaléta*
room	*dhiomátyo*	butli	*lúnyu*
...single/double	*monó/dhipló*	shower	*doos*
for three people	*ya tría átoma*	hot water	*zestó neró*
can I see it?	*boró na to dho?*	balcony	*balkóni*
breakfast	*proinó*	campsite	*kamping*
guest house	*pansyón*	key	*klidhí*
toilet paper	*charti iyías*	towel	*petséta*

bank	*trápeza*	exchange rate	*isotimía*
exchange office	*ghrafío sinalághmatos*	credit card	*pistotikí kárta*
post office	*tahidhrómio*	travellers' cheque	*taxidhyotikí epitayí*
money	*leftá*	passport	*dhiavatíryo*
cash desk	*tamío*	can I pay by...	*boró na plíróso me...*
how much	*póso káni*	cheap/expensive	*ftinós/akrivós*

restaurant	*estiatório*	bread	*psomi*
café	*kafenío*	water	*nero*
menu	*menóo*	wine	*krasi*
lunch	*yévma*	coffee	*kafés*
dinner	*dhípno*	fruit	*fróoto*
dessert	*epidhórpyo*	waitress	*servitóra*
waiter	*garsóni*	tea (black)	*tsái*
the bill	*loghariazmós*		

aeroplane	*aeropláno*	...single/return	*apló/metepistrofís*
airport	*aerodhrómio*	car	*aftokínito*
bus	*leoforío*	taxi	*taxí*
...station	*stathmós*	the road to...	*o dhrómos ya*
...stop	*stási*	no smoking	*mi kapnízondes*
boat	*karávi*	timetable	*dhromolóyo*
...port/harbour	*limáni*	petrol	*venzíni*
ticket	*isitírio*		

yes	*né*	goodbye	*....adío or yásas, yásoo*
no	*óhi*		
please	*parakaló*	sorry	*signómi*
thank you	*efharistó*	how much?	*póso káni?*
hello	*yásas, yásoo*	where is...?	*poú eené..?*
good morning	*kalí méra*	help!	*voíthia!*
good evening	*kalí spéra*	my name is...	*meh léne*
good night	*kalí níkhta*	I don't speak Greek	*then miló helliniká*
I don't understand	*thén katalavéno*	excuse me	*me sinchoríte*

REMEMBER

- Contact the airport, airline or travel representative 72 hours prior to leaving to ensure flights are unchanged.
- Arrive 90 minutes before your scheduled flight departure time, particularly in high season. Make sure you have all necessary documentation ready.
- Antiquities may not be taken out of Crete.

Index

TwinPack
Crete

Written by Susie Boulton
Contributions and additional writing by Tony Fennymore and Tim Powell
Designed and produced by AA Publishing
Editorial Management by Apostrophe S Limited
Series editor Cathy Hatley

A CIP catalogue record for this book is available from the British Library.

ISBN 978-0-7495-5171-1

Material in this book may have appeared in other AA publications.

Published by AA Publishing, a trading name of Automobile Association Developments Limited, whose registered office is Fanum House, Basing View, Basingstoke, Hampshire, RG21 4EA. Registered number 1878835.

Colour separation by Keenes, Andover
Printed and bound by Everbest Printing Co Limited, China

ACKNOWLEDGEMENTS
The Automobile Association wishes to thank the following photographers, companies and picture libraries for their assistance in the preparation of this book.

Abbreviations for the picture credits are as follows – (t) top; (b) bottom; (l) left; (r) right; (c) centre; (AA) AA World Travel Library; (F/C) Front Cover; (B/C) Back Cover

F/C i AA/K Paterson; F/C ii AA/W Voysey; F/C iii AA/K Paterson; F/C iv AA/K Paterson; F/C v AA/K Paterson; F/C vi AA/K Paterson; F/C vii AA/P Enticknap; F/C viii AA/K Paterson; F/C background AA/P Enticknap; B/C t AA/K Paterson; B/C ct Photodisc; B/C cb AA/C Sawyer; B/C b Brand X Pics; 1 AA; 5t AA/N Hicks; 5b AA/K Paterson; 6 AA/K Paterson; 7t AA/K Paterson, 7b AAP Enticknap; 8 AA/K Paterson; 9 AA/K Paterson; 12 AA/P Enticknap; 13t AA/K Paterson; 13b AA/P Enticknap; 14 AA/K Paterson; 15 AA/K Paterson; 16 AA/N Hicks; 17 AA/K Paterson; 18 AA/K Paterson; 19 AA/K Paterson; 20c AA/K Paterson; 20b AA/N Hicks; 21 AA/K Paterson; 23t AA/N Hicks; 23b AA/W Voysey; 24t AA/P Enticknap; 24b AA/K Paterson; 25t AA/K Patersonl 25b AA/N Hicks; 26t AA/K Paterson; 26b AA/P Enticknap; 27t AA/P Enticknap; 27b AA/P Enticknap; 28t AA/P Enticknap; 28b AA; 29t AA/K Paterson; 29b AA/P Enticknap; 30 AA/K Paterson; 31t AA/P Enticknap; 31b AA/P Enticknap; 32t Hilary Weston; 32b Hilary Weston; 33t AA/K Paterson; 33b AA/K Paterson; 34t AA/N Hicks; 34b AA/P Enticknap; 35t AA/N Hicks; 35c AA/K Paterson; 36t AA/N Hicks; 36c AA/K Paterson; 37t AA/P Enticknap; 37b AA/P Enticknap; 38t AA/N Hicks; 38c AA; 39t AA/K Paterson; 39b AA/K Paterson; 40t AA/N Hicks; 40b AA/N Hicks; 41t AA/P Enticknap; 41c AA/K Paterson; 42t AA/K Paterson; 42b AA/P Enticknap; 43t AA/K Paterson; 43b AA/K Paterson; 44t AA/K Paterson; 44b AA/N Hicks; 45t AA/K Paterson; 45b AA; 46t AA/P Enticknap; 46b AA/N Hicks; 47t AA/P Enticknap; 47b AA/K Paterson; 48t AA/K Paterson; 48b AA/K Paterson; 49t AA/P Enticknap; 49b AA/P Enticknap; 50 AA/K Paterson; 51 AA/N Hicks; 52 AA/K Paterson; 53 AA/N Hicks; 54 AA/P Enticknap; 55 AA/N Hicks; 57 AA/N Hicks; 58 AA/K Paterson; 60 AA/N Hicks; 61 AA/K Paterson; 62 AA/K Paterson; 63t AA/K Paterson; 63b AA/K Paterson; 84 AA/K Paterson; 85t AA/K Paterson; 85b AA/K Paterson; 90t AA/N Hicks; 90cl AA/T Harris; 90cr AA/N Hicks

Every effort has been made to trace the copyright holders, and we apologise in advance for any unintentional omissions or errors. We would be pleased to apply any corrections in any following edition of this publication.

A02961
Cover maps produced from mapping © Freytag-Berndt u. Artaria KG, 1231 Vienna-Austria
Fold out map © Freytag-Berndt u. Artaria KG, 1231 Vienna-Austria

TITLES IN THE TWINPACK SERIES
• Algarve • Corfu • Costa Blanca • Costa del Sol • Crete • Croatia • Cyprus • Gran Canaria •
• Lanzarote & Fuerteventura • Madeira • Mallorca • Malta & Gozo • Menorca • Tenerife •

Dear **TwinPack** Traveller

**Your comments, opinions and recommendations are very important to us.
So please help us to improve our travel guides by taking a few
minutes to complete this simple questionnaire.**

*You do not need a stamp (unless posted outside the UK). If you do not want to cut this page from your
guide, then photocopy it or write your answers on a plain sheet of paper.*

Send to: **The Editor, AA TwinPack Travel Guides,
FREEPOST SCE 4598, Basingstoke RG21 4GY.**

Your recommendations…

We always encourage readers' recommendations for restaurants, nightlife or shopping – if
your recommendation is used in the next edition of the guide, we will send you a *FREE*
AA TwinPack Guide of your choice. Please state below the establishment name,
location and your reasons for recommending it.

_____

_____

_____

_____

Please send me **AA TwinPack**

Algarve ☐ Corfu ☐ Costa Blanca ☐ Costa del Sol ☐ Crete ☐
Croatia ☐ Cyprus ☐ Gran Canaria ☐ Lanzarote & Fuerteventura ☐
Madeira ☐ Mallorca ☐ Malta & Gozo ☐ Menorca ☐ Tenerife ☐
(*please tick as appropriate*)

About this guide…

Which title did you buy?
AA *TwinPack* _____
Where did you buy it? _____
When? m m / y y

Why did you choose an AA *TwinPack* Guide? _____

_____

_____

_____

_____

Did this guide meet your expectations?
Exceeded ☐ Met all ☐ Met most ☐ Fell below ☐
Please give your reasons _____

_____

_____

continued on next page…

Were there any aspects of this guide that you particularly liked? _____

_____

_____

Is there anything we could have done better? _____

_____

_____

About you…

Name (*Mr/Mrs/Ms*) _____

Address _____

_____

_____ Postcode _____

Daytime tel no _____

Please only give us your mobile phone number if you wish to hear from us about other products and services from the AA and partners by text or mms.

Which age group are you in?

Under 25 ❑   25–34 ❑   35–44 ❑   45–54 ❑   55–64 ❑   65+ ❑

How many trips do you make a year?

Less than one ❑   One ❑   Two ❑   Three or more ❑

Are you an AA member? Yes ❑   No ❑

About your trip…

When did you book? m m / y y   When did you travel? m m / y y

How long did you stay? _____

Was it for business or leisure? _____

Did you buy any other travel guides for your trip?

If yes, which ones? _____

Thank you for taking the time to complete this questionnaire. Please send it to us as soon as possible, and remember, you do not need a stamp (*unless posted outside the UK*).

Happy Holidays!